THIS BOOK BELONGS TO

_____

START DATE

_____

SHE READS TRUTH

EXECUTIVE

FOUNDER/CHIEF EXECUTIVE OFFICER
Raechel Myers

CO-FOUNDER/CHIEF CONTENT OFFICER
Amanda Bible Williams

CHIEF OPERATING OFFICER
Ryan Myers

EXECUTIVE ASSISTANT
Sarah Andereck

EDITORIAL

INTERIM CONTENT DIRECTOR
Jessica Lamb

CONTENT EDITOR
Kara Gause

ASSOCIATE EDITORS
Bailey Gillespie
Ellen Taylor

EDITORIAL ASSISTANT
Hannah Little

CREATIVE

CREATIVE DIRECTOR
Jeremy Mitchell

LEAD DESIGNER
Kelsea Allen

DESIGNERS
Abbey Benson
Davis DeLisi
Annie Glover

MARKETING

MARKETING DIRECTOR
Hannah Warren

MARKETING MANAGER
Katie Pierce

SOCIAL MEDIA MANAGER
Ansley Rushing

COMMUNITY SUPPORT SPECIALIST
Margot Williams

SHIPPING & LOGISTICS

LOGISTICS MANAGER
Lauren Gloyne

SHIPPING MANAGER
Sydney Bess

CUSTOMER SUPPORT SPECIALIST
Katy McKnight

FULFILLMENT SPECIALISTS
Abigail Achord
Cait Baggerman
Kamiren Passavanti

SUBSCRIPTION INQUIRIES
orders@shereadstruth.com

CONTRIBUTOR

CONTENT
John Greco, MDiv

@SHEREADSTRUTH

Download the
She Reads Truth app,
available for iOS
and Android.

Subscribe to the
She Reads Truth podcast

SHEREADSTRUTH.COM

Research support provided by Logos Bible Software™. Learn more at logos.com.

Though the dates in this book have been carefully researched, scholars disagree on the dating of many biblical events.

This book was printed offset in Nashville, Tennessee, on 70# Lynx Opaque. Cover is 100# Cougar Opaque with a soft touch lamination.

DANIEL

We, too, are exiles in this world, longing for the day when we will live at home in the presence of Christ our King.

Amanda

Amanda Bible Williams
CO-FOUNDER & CHIEF
CONTENT OFFICER

Last week my husband called to say goodbye to his 94-year-old grandmother. Her body is showing signs of fatigue, and her doctors have said she doesn't have much time left. More than that, she can just sense it somehow.

He relayed the conversation to me afterward—how he told her would miss her, and how she said she loved him and called him "Doo-bug," the name she gave him when he was a baby. I listened, the familiar ache in my chest of knowing that our time here is temporary, though we like to pretend it isn't. What must it feel like, knowing the transition to heaven is near—to look back over nearly a century of celebration and sorrow, wars and babies, grandchildren and church potlucks and conversations on the front porch? What does success look like from that vantage point? What does it mean to live a faithful life?

In the book of Daniel, we get an overview of one man's life. This true story begins with Daniel being taken into captivity by the Babylonians, who desire to change everything about Daniel, from his name to the god he worships. The book recounts Daniel's roughly seventy years in exile. He will be a prophet, an interpreter of dreams, and a prisoner. He will fast, worship, and pray to the God of Israel under threat of his life. He'll survive a den of hungry lions by Yahweh's power and presence, and prophesy the glory of God's eternal kingdom. And while we know Daniel was not perfect—he was human, a sinner in need of grace—we'll get glimpses over these twelve chapters of what it looks like to live a faithful life in exile.

We, too, are exiles in this world, longing for the day when we will live at home in the presence of Christ our King. We are citizens of heaven, but we take up residence here for a time, called to represent God's image on every stretch of the journey. As we wrestle with what it looks like to live a faithful life, we look past Daniel to the perfection of Jesus Christ. He is our example and advocate, our just judge and righteous ruler.

This book was carefully compiled to give context to Daniel's story and guide you through its abundant imagery and symbolism. The daily worksheets are helpful study tools, and the timeline on page 60 is thoughtfully designed and informative. My favorite extra is "The Son of Man," found on page 72. Our team put so much love and care into this resource, and we pray it grows your affection for our gracious, good, and sovereign God as you read.

Long live the King.

At She Reads Truth, we believe in pairing the inherently beautiful Word of God with the aesthetic beauty it deserves. Each of our resources is thoughtfully and artfully designed to highlight the beauty, goodness, and truth of Scripture in a way that reflects the themes of each curated reading plan.

For the images in this Study Book, we created linear patterns in white paint and spackling paste. These images reflect the journeys of those who were loyal to God and persevered in response to His faithfulness and love.

We incorporated type design with thin lines and shapes on many spreads in this book to further represent the peaks and valleys experienced by God's people in the book of Daniel.

She Reads Truth is a community of women dedicated to reading the Word of God every day.

The Bible is living and active, breathed out by God, and we confidently hold it higher than anything we can do or say. This book focuses primarily on Scripture, with bonus resources to facilitate deeper engagement with God's Word.

SCRIPTURE READING

Designed for a Monday start, this Study Book presents the book of Daniel in daily readings, with supplemental passages for additional context.

WORKSHEETS

Each weekday includes an interactive worksheet to guide you as you read.

GRACE DAY

Use Saturdays to catch up on your reading, pray, and rest in the presence of the Lord.

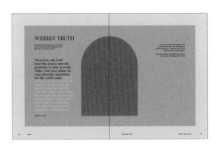

WEEKLY TRUTH

Sundays are set aside for Scripture memorization.

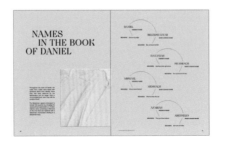

EXTRAS

This book features additional tools to help you gain a deeper understanding of the text.

Devotionals corresponding to each daily reading can be found in the **Daniel** reading plan at SheReadsTruth.com or on the She Reads Truth app. We invite you to join women from Portland to Poland in conversation and community as you read along.

⟨ PLANS

Daniel

3 Weeks

PLAN OVERVIEW

A Jewish exile in Babylon, Daniel sought to honor God even as he lived in a land of false gods and under the rule of foreign kings. This book of prophecy and historical narrative is one of dreams and visions, persecution and identity. But even more, it is a story of how God is the King whose dominion is not shaken even in the most dire of circumstances. Join us in a three-week study of the book of Daniel as

Day 1 **Daniel's Captivity in Babylon**

Day 2 **Faithfulness in Babylon**

TABLE OF CON- TENTS

WK 1

WK 2

WK 3

SHE READS DANIEL

FOR HIS DOMINION IS AN EVERLASTING DOMINION, AND HIS KINGDOM IS FROM GENERATION TO GENERATION.

ON THE TIMELINE

The events in the book of Daniel took place between 605 and 535 BC, during the time of the nation of Judah's Babylonian captivity. The book opens after King Nebuchadnezzar's first siege of Judah in 605 BC, when he brought Daniel—along with other captives from the Judean nobility—to Babylon. Nebuchadnezzar's assault of Judah continued in 597 and 586 BC, and each time the number of his prisoners grew. Daniel's ministry began when he arrived in Babylon with those first captives, extended throughout the Babylonian captivity, and concluded after the third year of Cyrus the Great, the Medo-Persian king who overthrew Babylon in 539 BC (Dn 1:21; 10:1).

A LITTLE BACKGROUND

Tradition maintains that the prophet Daniel wrote this book sometime shortly after the end of the Babylonian captivity. The book contains retellings of events in his life as well as supernatural predictions of events that would take place during the intertestamental period. Daniel is written to the Jewish exiles in Babylon to remind them of God's sovereignty and encourage them to remain faithful to God even amid their difficult circumstances.

MESSAGE AND PURPOSE

The theme of the book of Daniel is the hope of God's people during "the times of the Gentiles," a phrase used by Jesus to refer to the time between the Babylonian captivity and Jesus's return (Lk 21:24). Though it was a lengthy time when God's people lived under ungodly rule, the book of Daniel offers hope in its teaching that, at all times, "the Most High God is ruler over human kingdoms" (Dn 5:21). To encourage Israel's faithfulness to its sovereign God, Daniel recounted examples of godly trust and delivered prophecies of God's ultimate victory.

GIVE THANKS FOR THE BOOK OF DANIEL

Above all, Daniel teaches that the God of Israel is the sovereign God of the universe, "for his dominion is an everlasting dominion, and his kingdom is from generation to generation" (Dn 4:34). Even when wicked empires have extensive reign, the prophet's words remind us that only the Lord has dominion over all the kingdoms of the earth.

Tips for Reading the Book of Daniel

The book of Daniel is a combination of narrative (ch. 1–6) and apocalyptic literature (ch. 7–12).

While narrative recounts connected events, apocalyptic literature recounts a vision or dream. The visions in Daniel contain symbols and imagery that communicate literal truth about the past, present, and future.

The events in Daniel are not always linear. The book contains flashbacks and flashforwards and encompasses most of Daniel's life.

As you read, remember that the events in Daniel happened to real people living in an actual place.

Keep in mind that the book had an original audience with a different context for the symbolism in the apocalyptic sections of the book.

DANIEL'S CAPTIVITY IN BABYLON

Daniel 1:1–7

DANIEL'S CAPTIVITY IN BABYLON

[1] In the third year of the reign of King Jehoiakim of Judah, King Nebuchadnezzar of Babylon came to Jerusalem and laid siege to it. [2] The Lord handed King Jehoiakim of Judah over to him, along with some of the vessels from the house of God. Nebuchadnezzar carried them to the land of Babylon, to the house of his god, and put the vessels in the treasury of his god.

[3] The king ordered Ashpenaz, his chief eunuch, to bring some of the Israelites from the royal family and from the nobility— [4] young men without any physical defect, good-looking, suitable for instruction in all wisdom, knowledgeable, perceptive, and capable of serving in the king's palace. He was to teach them the Chaldean language and literature. [5] The king assigned them daily provisions from the royal food and from the wine that he drank. They were to be trained for three years, and at the end of that time they were to attend the king. [6] Among them, from the Judahites, were Daniel, Hananiah, Mishael, and Azariah. [7] The chief eunuch gave them names; he gave the name Belteshazzar to Daniel, Shadrach to Hananiah, Meshach to Mishael, and Abednego to Azariah.

2 Kings 24:10–17

DEPORTATIONS TO BABYLON

[10] At that time the servants of King Nebuchadnezzar of Babylon marched up to Jerusalem, and the city came under siege. [11] King Nebuchadnezzar of Babylon came to the city while his servants were besieging it. [12] King Jehoiachin of Judah, along with his mother, his servants, his commanders, and his officials, surrendered to the king of Babylon.

So the king of Babylon took him captive in the eighth year of his reign. [13] He also carried off from there all the treasures of the LORD's temple and the treasures of the king's palace, and he cut into pieces all the gold articles that King Solomon of Israel had made for the LORD's sanctuary, just as the LORD had predicted. [14] He deported all Jerusalem and all the commanders and all the best soldiers— ten thousand captives including all the craftsmen and metalsmiths. Except for the poorest people of the land, no one remained.

[15] Nebuchadnezzar deported Jehoiachin to Babylon. He took the king's mother, the king's wives, his officials, and the leading men of the land into exile from Jerusalem to Babylon. [16] The king of Babylon brought captive into Babylon all seven thousand of the best soldiers and one thousand craftsmen and metalsmiths— all strong and fit for war. [17] And the king of Babylon made Mattaniah, Jehoiachin's uncle, king in his place and changed his name to Zedekiah.

Psalm 137:1–6

LAMENT OF THE EXILES

[1] By the rivers of Babylon—
there we sat down and wept
when we remembered Zion.
[2] There we hung up our lyres
on the poplar trees,
[3] for our captors there asked us for songs,
and our tormentors, for rejoicing:
"Sing us one of the songs of Zion."

[4] How can we sing the LORD's song
on foreign soil?
[5] If I forget you, Jerusalem,
may my right hand forget its skill.
[6] May my tongue stick to the roof of my mouth
if I do not remember you,
if I do not exalt Jerusalem as my greatest joy!

Day:	Reading:

NARRATIVE

TODAY'S READING WAS
(circle one)

A DREAM

The main symbol was

○ A COLOSSAL STATUE

○ A TALL TREE

The Ruler

○ King Nebuchadnezzar of Babylon

○ King Belshazzar of Babylon

○ Darius the Mede

○ King Cyrus of Persia

POINT OF VIEW

○ THIRD PERSON

○ FIRST PERSON

Speaker:

_____

Mentioned by name

○ God

○ Daniel

○ Shadrach

○ Meshach

○ Abednego

○ Chaldeans

○ The Queen

○ Ancient of Days

○ Son of Man

○ Gabriel

○ Michael

What was the

CENTRAL CONFLICT

_____

RESOLUTION

Describe the actions, habits, and attitudes of the Babylonian captors and the Hebrew captives.

NAMES IN THE BOOK OF DANIEL

Throughout the book of Daniel, the exiles from Judah were faced with questions about their identity. Since they had been captured by the Babylonians and no longer lived in the promised land, were they still the people of God?

The Babylonian captors attempted to answer this question by changing the names of their captives (Dn 1:1–7). Each Hebrew name containing a reference to the true God was replaced with a Babylonian counterpart alluding to a Babylonian deity.

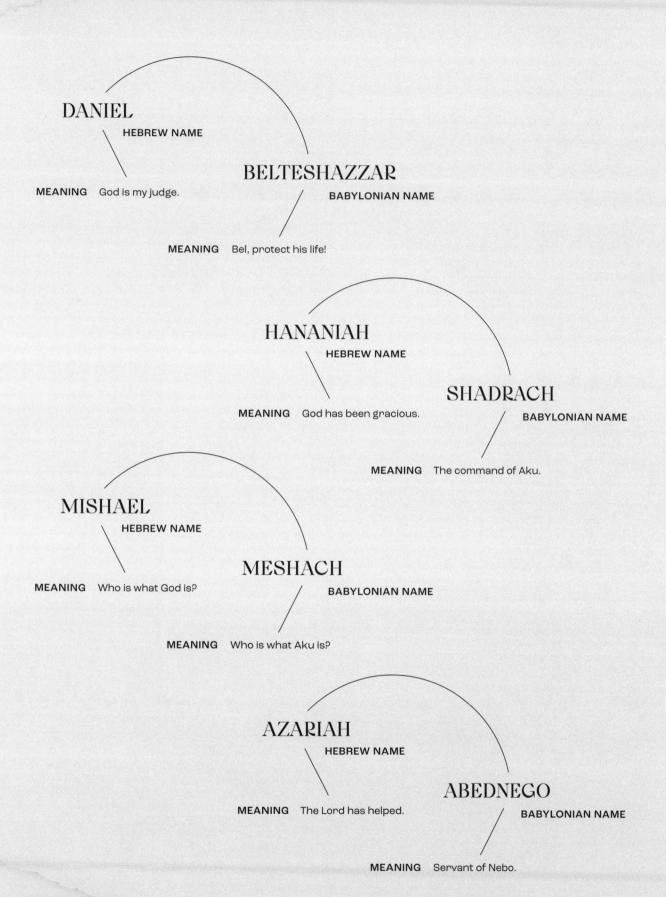

DANIEL

HEBREW NAME

MEANING   God is my judge.

BELTESHAZZAR

BABYLONIAN NAME

MEANING   Bel, protect his life!

HANANIAH

HEBREW NAME

MEANING   God has been gracious.

SHADRACH

BABYLONIAN NAME

MEANING   The command of Aku.

MISHAEL

HEBREW NAME

MEANING   Who is what God is?

MESHACH

BABYLONIAN NAME

MEANING   Who is what Aku is?

AZARIAH

HEBREW NAME

MEANING   The Lord has helped.

ABEDNEGO

BABYLONIAN NAME

MEANING   Servant of Nebo.

FAITHFULNESS

 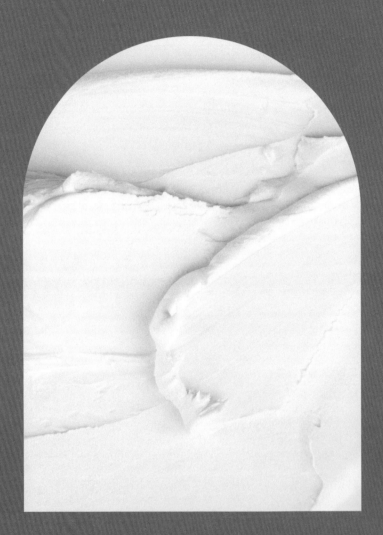

IN BABYLON

Daniel 1:8–21

FAITHFULNESS IN BABYLON

[8] Daniel determined that he would not defile himself with the king's food or with the wine he drank. So he asked permission from the chief eunuch not to defile himself. [9] God had granted Daniel kindness and compassion from the chief eunuch, [10] yet he said to Daniel, "I fear my lord the king, who assigned your food and drink. What if he sees your faces looking thinner than the other young men your age? You would endanger my life with the king."

[11] So Daniel said to the guard whom the chief eunuch had assigned to Daniel, Hananiah, Mishael, and Azariah, [12] "Please test your servants for ten days. Let us be given vegetables to eat and water to drink. [13] Then examine our appearance and the appearance of the young men who are eating the king's food, and deal with your servants based on what you see." [14] He agreed with them about this and tested them for ten days. [15] At the end of ten days they looked better and healthier than all the young men who were eating the king's food. [16] So the guard continued to remove their food and the wine they were to drink and gave them vegetables.

FAITHFULNESS REWARDED

[17] God gave these four young men knowledge and understanding in every kind of literature and wisdom.

Daniel also understood visions and dreams of every kind.

[18] At the end of the time that the king had said to present them, the chief eunuch presented them to Nebuchadnezzar. [19] The king interviewed them, and among all of them, no one was found equal to Daniel, Hananiah, Mishael, and Azariah. So they began to attend the king. [20] In every matter of wisdom and understanding that the king consulted them about, he found them ten times better than all the magicians and mediums in his entire kingdom. [21] Daniel remained there until the first year of King Cyrus.

1 Samuel 12:24

Above all, fear the LORD and worship him faithfully with all your heart; consider the great things he has done for you.

1 Peter 2:11-17

[11] Dear friends, I urge you as strangers and exiles to abstain from sinful desires that wage war against the soul. [12] Conduct yourselves honorably among the Gentiles, so that when they slander you as evildoers, they will observe your good works and will glorify God on the day he visits.

[13] Submit to every human authority because of the Lord, whether to the emperor as the supreme authority [14] or to governors as those sent out by him to punish those who do what is evil and to praise those who do what is good.

[15] For it is God's will that you silence the ignorance of foolish people by doing good.

[16] Submit as free people, not using your freedom as a cover-up for evil, but as God's slaves. [17] Honor everyone. Love the brothers and sisters. Fear God. Honor the emperor.

Day:	Reading:

NARRATIVE

TODAY'S READING WAS
(circle one)

A DREAM

The main symbol was

○ A COLOSSAL STATUE

○ A TALL TREE

The Ruler

○ King Nebuchadnezzar of Babylon

○ King Belshazzar of Babylon

○ Darius the Mede

○ King Cyrus of Persia

POINT OF VIEW

○ THIRD PERSON

○ FIRST PERSON

Speaker:

_____

Mentioned by name

○ God

○ Daniel

○ Shadrach

○ Meshach

○ Abednego

○ Chaldeans

○ The Queen

○ Ancient of Days

○ Son of Man

○ Gabriel

○ Michael

What was the

CENTRAL CONFLICT

_____

RESOLUTION

List things said about God or actions that He takes.

DAY 03

NEBUCHADNEZZAR'S DREAM

Daniel 2:1–24

NEBUCHADNEZZAR'S DREAM

¹ In the second year of his reign, Nebuchadnezzar had dreams that troubled him, and sleep deserted him. ² So the king gave orders to summon the magicians, mediums, sorcerers, and Chaldeans to tell the king his dreams. When they came and stood before the king, ³ he said to them, "I have had a dream and am anxious to understand it."

⁴ The Chaldeans spoke to the king (Aramaic begins here): "May the king live forever. Tell your servants the dream, and we will give the interpretation."

⁵ The king replied to the Chaldeans, "My word is final: If you don't tell me the dream and its interpretation, you will be torn limb from limb, and your houses will be made a garbage dump. ⁶ But if you make the dream and its interpretation known to me, you'll receive gifts, a reward, and great honor from me. So make the dream and its interpretation known to me."

[7] They answered a second time, "May the king tell the dream to his servants, and we will make known the interpretation."

[8] The king replied, "I know for certain you are trying to gain some time, because you see that my word is final. [9] If you don't tell me the dream, there is one decree for you. You have conspired to tell me something false or fraudulent until the situation changes. So tell me the dream and I will know you can give me its interpretation."

[10] The Chaldeans answered the king, "No one on earth can make known what the king requests. Consequently, no king, however great and powerful, has ever asked anything like this of any magician, medium, or Chaldean. [11] What the king is asking is so difficult that no one can make it known to him except the gods, whose dwelling is not with mortals." [12] Because of this, the king became violently angry and gave orders to destroy all the wise men of Babylon. [13] The decree was issued that the wise men were to be executed, and they searched for Daniel and his friends, to execute them.

[14] Then Daniel responded with tact and discretion to Arioch, the captain of the king's guard, who had gone out to execute the wise men of Babylon. [15] He asked Arioch, the king's officer, "Why is the decree from the king so harsh?" Then Arioch explained the situation to Daniel. [16] So Daniel went and asked the king to give him some time, so that he could give the king the interpretation.

[17] Then Daniel went to his house and told his friends Hananiah, Mishael, and Azariah about the matter, [18] urging them to ask the God of the heavens for mercy concerning this mystery, so Daniel and his friends would not be destroyed with the rest of Babylon's wise men. [19] The mystery was then revealed to Daniel in a vision at night, and Daniel praised the God of the heavens [20] and declared:

> May the name of God
> be praised forever and ever,
> for wisdom and power belong to him.
> [21] He changes the times and seasons;
> he removes kings and establishes kings.
> He gives wisdom to the wise
> and knowledge to those
> who have understanding.
> [22] He reveals the deep and hidden things;
> he knows what is in the darkness,
> and light dwells with him.
> [23] I offer thanks and praise to you,
> God of my ancestors,

because you have given me
wisdom and power.
And now you have let me know
what we asked of you,
for you have let us know
the king's mystery.

²⁴ Therefore Daniel went to Arioch, whom the king had assigned to destroy the wise men of Babylon. He came and said to him, "Don't destroy the wise men of Babylon! Bring me before the king, and I will give him the interpretation."

Psalm 145:1–2

¹ I exalt you, my God the King,
and bless your name forever and ever.
² I will bless you every day;
I will praise your name forever and ever.

Isaiah 44:6–8

⁶ This is what the Lord, the King of Israel and its Redeemer, the Lord of Armies, says:

I am the first and I am the last.
There is no God but me.
⁷ Who, like me, can announce
the future?

Let him say so and make a case before me,
since I have established an ancient people.
Let these gods declare the coming things,
and what will take place.
⁸ Do not be startled or afraid.
Have I not told you and declared it long ago?
You are my witnesses!
Is there any God but me?
There is no other Rock; I do not know any.

Day:	Reading:

NARRATIVE

TODAY'S READING WAS
(circle one)

A DREAM

The main symbol was

○ A COLOSSAL STATUE

○ A TALL TREE

The Ruler

○ King Nebuchadnezzar of Babylon

○ King Belshazzar of Babylon

○ Darius the Mede

○ King Cyrus of Persia

POINT OF VIEW

○ THIRD PERSON

○ FIRST PERSON

Speaker:

_____

Mentioned by name

○ God

○ Daniel

○ Shadrach

○ Meshach

○ Abednego

○ Chaldeans

○ The Queen

○ Ancient of Days

○ Son of Man

○ Gabriel

○ Michael

What was the

CENTRAL CONFLICT

_____

RESOLUTION

Describe the actions, habits, and attitudes of the Babylonian captors and the Hebrew captives.

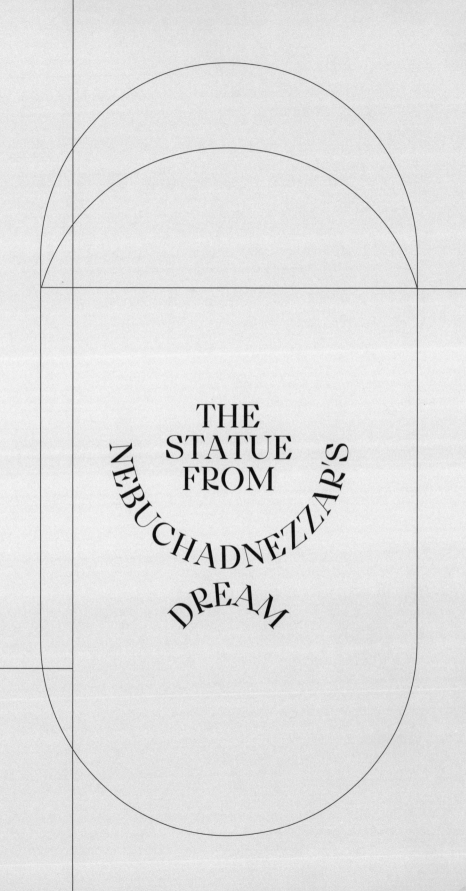

THE STATUE FROM NEBUCHADNEZZAR'S DREAM

HEAD OF GOLD

CHEST & ARMS OF SILVER

STOMACH & THIGHS
OF BRONZE

LEGS OF IRON

FEET OF IRON
& FIRED CLAY

DANIEL INTERPRETS

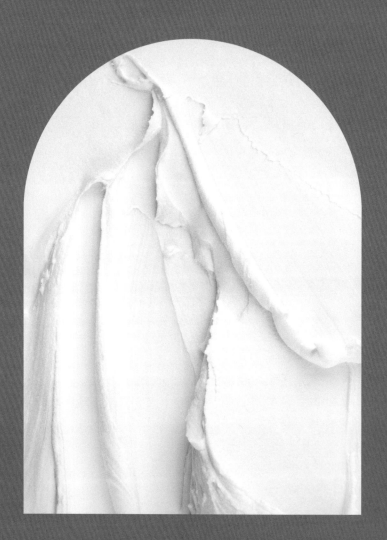

DAY   04

THE DREAM

Daniel 2:25–49

²⁵ Then Arioch quickly brought Daniel before the king and said to him, "I have found a man among the Judean exiles who can let the king know the interpretation."

²⁶ The king said in reply to Daniel, whose name was Belteshazzar, "Are you able to tell me the dream I had and its interpretation?"

²⁷ Daniel answered the king, "No wise man, medium, magician, or diviner is able to make known to the king the mystery he asked about.

²⁸ But there is a God in heaven who reveals mysteries,

and he has let King Nebuchadnezzar know what will happen in the last days. Your dream and the visions that came into your mind as you lay in bed were these: ²⁹ Your Majesty, while you were in your bed, thoughts came to your mind about what will happen in the future. The revealer of mysteries has let you know what will happen. ³⁰ As for me, this mystery has been revealed to me, not because I have more wisdom than anyone living, but in order that the interpretation might be made known to the king, and that you may understand the thoughts of your mind.

THE DREAM'S INTERPRETATION

³¹ "Your Majesty, as you were watching, suddenly a colossal statue appeared. That statue, tall and dazzling, was standing in front of you, and its appearance was terrifying. ³² The head of the statue was pure gold, its chest and arms were silver, its stomach and thighs were bronze, ³³ its legs were iron, and its feet were partly iron and partly fired clay. ³⁴ As you were watching, a stone broke off without a hand touching it, struck the statue on its feet of iron and fired clay, and crushed them. ³⁵ Then the iron, the fired clay, the bronze, the silver, and the gold were shattered and became like chaff from the summer threshing floors. The wind carried them away, and not a trace of them could be found. But the stone that struck the statue became a great mountain and filled the whole earth.

³⁶ "This was the dream; now we will tell the king its interpretation. ³⁷ Your Majesty, you are king of kings. The God of the heavens has given you sovereignty, power, strength, and glory. ³⁸ Wherever people live—or wild animals, or birds of the sky—he has handed them over to you and made you ruler over them all. You are the head of gold.

³⁹ "After you, there will arise another kingdom, inferior to yours, and then another, a third kingdom, of bronze, which will rule the whole earth. ⁴⁰ A fourth kingdom will be as strong as iron; for iron crushes and shatters everything, and like iron that

smashes, it will crush and smash all the others. [41] You saw the feet and toes, partly of a potter's fired clay and partly of iron—it will be a divided kingdom, though some of the strength of iron will be in it. You saw the iron mixed with clay, [42] and that the toes of the feet were partly iron and partly fired clay—part of the kingdom will be strong, and part will be brittle. [43] You saw the iron mixed with clay—the peoples will mix with one another but will not hold together, just as iron does not mix with fired clay.

[44] "In the days of those kings, the God of the heavens will set up a kingdom that will never be destroyed, and this kingdom will not be left to another people. It will crush all these kingdoms and bring them to an end, but will itself endure forever. [45] You saw a stone break off from the mountain without a hand touching it, and it crushed the iron, bronze, fired clay, silver, and gold. The great God has told the king what will happen in the future. The dream is certain, and its interpretation reliable."

NEBUCHADNEZZAR'S RESPONSE

[46] Then King Nebuchadnezzar fell facedown, worshiped Daniel, and gave orders to present an offering and incense to him. [47] The king said to Daniel, "Your God is indeed God of gods, Lord of kings, and a revealer of mysteries, since you were able to reveal this mystery." [48] Then the king promoted Daniel and gave him many generous gifts. He made him ruler over the entire province of Babylon and chief governor over all the wise men of Babylon. [49] At Daniel's request, the king appointed Shadrach, Meshach, and Abednego to manage the province of Babylon. But Daniel remained at the king's court.

Luke 12:8–12

[8] "And I say to you, anyone who acknowledges me before others, the Son of Man will also acknowledge him before the angels of God, [9] but whoever denies me before others will be denied before the angels of God. [10] Anyone who speaks a word against the Son of Man will be forgiven, but the one who blasphemes against the Holy Spirit will not be forgiven. [11] Whenever they bring you before synagogues and rulers and authorities, don't worry about how you should defend yourselves or what you should say. [12] For the Holy Spirit will teach you at that very hour what must be said."

1 Corinthians 15:24–27

[24] Then comes the end, when he hands over the kingdom to God the Father, when he abolishes all rule and all authority and power. [25] For he must reign until he puts all his enemies under his feet. [26] The last enemy to be abolished is death. [27] For God has put everything under his feet. Now when it says "everything" is put under him, it is obvious that he who puts everything under him is the exception.

Day:	Reading:

NARRATIVE

TODAY'S READING WAS
(circle one)

A DREAM

The main symbol was

○ A COLOSSAL STATUE

○ A TALL TREE

The Ruler

○ King Nebuchadnezzar of Babylon

○ King Belshazzar of Babylon

○ Darius the Mede

○ King Cyrus of Persia

POINT OF VIEW

○ THIRD PERSON

○ FIRST PERSON

Speaker:

_____

Mentioned by name

○ God

○ Daniel

○ Shadrach

○ Meshach

○ Abednego

○ Chaldeans

○ The Queen

○ Ancient of Days

○ Son of Man

○ Gabriel

○ Michael

What was the

CENTRAL CONFLICT

_____

RESOLUTION

List things said about God or actions that He takes.

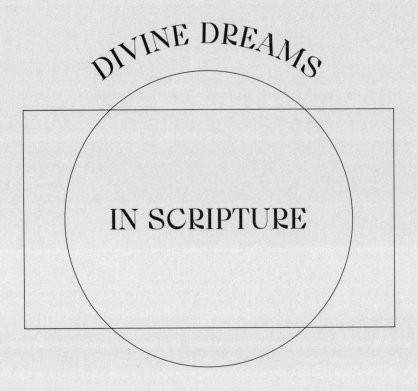

DIVINE DREAMS

IN SCRIPTURE

Daniel also understood visions
and dreams of every kind.

DANIEL 1:17

Daniel had a God-given ability to accurately interpret visions and dreams. Throughout Scripture, God used dreams and visions to reveal a truth, communicate His will, or explain events, particularly to His prophets (Nm 12:6). Visions typically occurred when people were awake, and prophetic dreams took place while people were sleeping. On the following pages are twenty dreams recorded in the Bible.

20 DREAMS

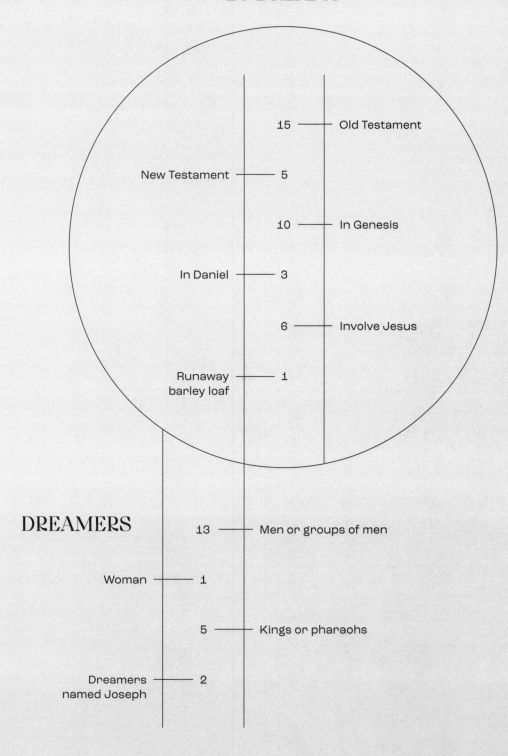

15 — Old Testament

New Testament — 5

10 — In Genesis

In Daniel — 3

6 — Involve Jesus

Runaway barley loaf — 1

DREAMERS

13 — Men or groups of men

Woman — 1

5 — Kings or pharaohs

Dreamers named Joseph — 2

OLD TESTAMENT

ABIMELECH'S DREAM

Abimelech receives a warning from God about sleeping with Sarah, Abraham's wife.

GN 20:3–7

JACOB'S DREAMS

Jacob dreams of a stairway between the ground and the sky, with angels going up and down from it. God confirms Jacob is the heir to God's promise to Abraham and Isaac.

GN 28:12–16

Jacob dreams about flocks of sheep, and God urges him to return to his native land.

GN 31:10–13

JOSEPH'S DREAMS

Joseph tells his brothers about a dream where their sheaves of grain bow to his.

GN 37:5–8

Joseph describes another dream to his brothers, where the sun, moon, and eleven stars bow down to him.

GN 37:9–10

LABAN'S DREAM

During his pursuit of Jacob, Laban is warned against saying anything good or bad to Jacob.

GN 31:22–24

THE CUPBEARER'S DREAM

Pharaoh's chief cupbearer dreams of a vine with three branches that blossom and ripen with grapes. Joseph tells the cupbearer that Pharaoh will restore his position in three days.

GN 40:5, 9–13

THE BAKER'S DREAM

Pharaoh's chief baker dreams he has three baskets of white bread for Pharaoh on his head, but birds are eating at the bread. Joseph tells the baker that in three days, Pharaoh will hang him on a tree.

GN 40:5, 16–19

PHARAOH'S DREAMS

Pharaoh dreams about seven sickly, thin cows eating seven healthy, well-fed cows. GN 41:1–4

Pharaoh dreams about seven thin, scorched heads of grain swallowing seven plump, good heads of grain.

GN 41:5–7

SOLOMON'S DREAM

The Lord appears to Solomon at Gibeon and tells him that he can ask for anything.

1KG 3:5–15

UNNAMED MIDIANITE'S DREAM

Gideon overhears a man telling his friend about a dream where a barley loaf took out a tent in their Midianite camp.

JDG 7:13

NEBUCHADNEZZAR'S DREAMS

Nebuchadnezzar has a troubling dream about a great statue, and Daniel interprets it as the destiny of his kingdom.

DN 2:1–45

DANIEL'S DREAM

Daniel dreams about four huge beasts, a little horn, and future kingdoms.

DN 7:1–28

Nebuchadnezzar has a dream about a tree being cut down, and Daniel interprets it as the king's fate until he acknowledges the Lord.

DN 4:4–27

NEW TESTAMENT

WISE MEN'S DREAM

After following the star to Jesus, the wise men are warned in a dream not to return to King Herod and to choose another route home.

MT 2:10–12

JOSEPH'S DREAMS

An angel of the Lord reassures Joseph that he can take Mary as his wife since the child in her womb is from the Holy Spirit.

MT 1:18–23

An angel of the Lord prompts Joseph to flee with Mary to Egypt in order to protect the Christ child from Herod.

MT 2:13–15

An angel of the Lord tells Joseph to return to Israel with his wife and child now that Herod is dead.

MT 2:19–21

PILATE'S WIFE'S DREAM

Pilate's wife has a terrible dream about Jesus and urges her husband to have nothing to do with that righteous man.

MT 27:15–19

DELIVERED FROM THE FIRE

Daniel 3

NEBUCHADNEZZAR'S GOLD STATUE

[1] King Nebuchadnezzar made a gold statue, ninety feet high and nine feet wide. He set it up on the plain of Dura in the province of Babylon. [2] King Nebuchadnezzar sent word to assemble the satraps, prefects, governors, advisers, treasurers, judges, magistrates, and all the rulers of the provinces to attend the dedication of the statue King Nebuchadnezzar had set up. [3] So the satraps, prefects, governors, advisers, treasurers, judges, magistrates, and all the rulers of the provinces assembled for the dedication of the statue the king had set up. Then they stood before the statue Nebuchadnezzar had set up.

[4] A herald loudly proclaimed, "People of every nation and language, you are commanded: [5] When you hear the sound of the horn, flute, zither, lyre, harp, drum, and every kind of music, you are to fall facedown and worship the gold statue that King Nebuchadnezzar has set up. [6] But whoever does not fall down and worship will immediately be thrown into a furnace of blazing fire."

7 Therefore, when all the people heard the sound of the horn, flute, zither, lyre, harp, and every kind of music, people of every nation and language fell down and worshiped the gold statue that King Nebuchadnezzar had set up.

THE FURNACE OF BLAZING FIRE

8 Some Chaldeans took this occasion to come forward and maliciously accuse the Jews. 9 They said to King Nebuchadnezzar, "May the king live forever. 10 You as king have issued a decree that everyone who hears the sound of the horn, flute, zither, lyre, harp, drum, and every kind of music must fall down and worship the gold statue. 11 Whoever does not fall down and worship will be thrown into a furnace of blazing fire. 12 There are some Jews you have appointed to manage the province of Babylon: Shadrach, Meshach, and Abednego. These men have ignored you, the king; they do not serve your gods or worship the gold statue you have set up."

13 Then in a furious rage Nebuchadnezzar gave orders to bring in Shadrach, Meshach, and Abednego. So these men were brought before the king. 14 Nebuchadnezzar asked them, "Shadrach, Meshach, and Abednego, is it true that you don't serve my gods or worship the gold statue I have set up? 15 Now if you're ready, when you hear the sound of the horn, flute, zither, lyre, harp, drum, and every kind of music, fall down and worship the statue I made. But if you don't worship it, you will immediately be thrown into a furnace of blazing fire—and who is the god who can rescue you from my power?"

16 Shadrach, Meshach, and Abednego replied to the king, "Nebuchadnezzar, we don't need to give you an answer to this question. 17 If the God we serve exists, then he can rescue us from the furnace of blazing fire, and he can rescue us from the power of you, the king.

18 But even if he does not rescue us, we want you as king to know that we will not serve your gods or worship the gold statue you set up."

19 Then Nebuchadnezzar was filled with rage, and the expression on his face changed toward Shadrach, Meshach, and Abednego. He gave orders to heat the furnace seven times more than was customary, 20 and he commanded some of the best soldiers in his army to tie up Shadrach, Meshach, and Abednego and throw them into the furnace of blazing fire. 21 So these men, in their trousers, robes, head coverings, and other clothes, were tied up and thrown into the furnace of blazing

fire. [22] Since the king's command was so urgent and the furnace extremely hot, the raging flames killed those men who carried up Shadrach, Meshach, and Abednego. [23] And these three men, Shadrach, Meshach, and Abednego fell, bound, into the furnace of blazing fire.

DELIVERED FROM THE FIRE

[24] Then King Nebuchadnezzar jumped up in alarm. He said to his advisers, "Didn't we throw three men, bound, into the fire?"

"Yes, of course, Your Majesty," they replied to the king.

[25] He exclaimed, "Look! I see four men, not tied, walking around in the fire unharmed; and the fourth looks like a son of the gods."

[26] Nebuchadnezzar then approached the door of the furnace of blazing fire and called, "Shadrach, Meshach, and Abednego, you servants of the Most High God—come out!" So Shadrach, Meshach, and Abednego came out of the fire. [27] When the satraps, prefects, governors, and the king's advisers gathered around, they saw that the fire had no effect on the bodies of these men: not a hair of their heads was singed, their robes were unaffected, and there was no smell of fire on them. [28] Nebuchadnezzar exclaimed, "Praise to the God of Shadrach, Meshach, and Abednego! He sent his angel and rescued his servants who trusted in him. They violated the king's command and risked their lives rather than serve or worship any god except their own God. [29] Therefore I issue a decree that anyone of any people, nation, or language who says anything offensive against the God of Shadrach, Meshach, and Abednego will be torn limb from limb and his house made a garbage dump. For there is no other god who is able to deliver like this." [30] Then the king rewarded Shadrach, Meshach, and Abednego in the province of Babylon.

Psalm 27

MY STRONGHOLD

Of David.

[1] The LORD is my light and my salvation—
whom should I fear?
The LORD is the stronghold of my life—
whom should I dread?
[2] When evildoers came against me to devour my flesh,
my foes and my enemies stumbled and fell.
[3] Though an army deploys against me,
my heart will not be afraid;
though a war breaks out against me,
I will still be confident.

⁴ I have asked one thing from the Lord;
it is what I desire:
to dwell in the house of the Lord
all the days of my life,
gazing on the beauty of the Lord
and seeking him in his temple.
⁵ For he will conceal me in his shelter
in the day of adversity;
he will hide me under the cover of his tent;
he will set me high on a rock.
⁶ Then my head will be high
above my enemies around me;
I will offer sacrifices in his tent with shouts of joy.
I will sing and make music to the Lord.

⁷ Lord, hear my voice when I call;
be gracious to me and answer me.
⁸ My heart says this about you:
"Seek his face."
Lord, I will seek your face.
⁹ Do not hide your face from me;
do not turn your servant away in anger.
You have been my helper;
do not leave me or abandon me,
God of my salvation.
¹⁰ Even if my father and mother abandon me,
the Lord cares for me.

¹¹ Because of my adversaries,
show me your way, Lord,
and lead me on a level path.
¹² Do not give me over to the will of my foes,
for false witnesses rise up against me,
breathing violence.

¹³ I am certain that I will see the Lord's goodness
in the land of the living.
¹⁴ Wait for the Lord;
be strong, and let your heart be courageous.
Wait for the Lord.

Isaiah 43:2

When you pass through the waters,
I will be with you,
and the rivers will not overwhelm you.
When you walk through the fire,
you will not be scorched,
and the flame will not burn you.

Day:	Reading:

NARRATIVE

TODAY'S READING WAS
(circle one)

A DREAM

The main symbol was

○ A COLOSSAL STATUE

○ A TALL TREE

The Ruler

○ King Nebuchadnezzar of Babylon

○ King Belshazzar of Babylon

○ Darius the Mede

○ King Cyrus of Persia

POINT OF VIEW

○ THIRD PERSON

○ FIRST PERSON

Speaker:

_____

Mentioned by name

○ God

○ Daniel

○ Shadrach

○ Meshach

○ Abednego

○ Chaldeans

○ The Queen

○ Ancient of Days

○ Son of Man

○ Gabriel

○ Michael

What was the

CENTRAL CONFLICT

_____

RESOLUTION

Describe the actions, habits, and attitudes of the Babylonian captors and the Hebrew captives.

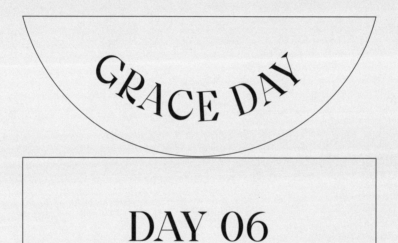

GRACE DAY

DAY 06

Take this day to catch up on your reading, pray, and rest in the presence of the Lord.

Above all, fear the Lord and worship him faithfully with all your heart; consider the great things he has done for you.

1 SAMUEL 12:24

WEEKLY TRUTH

Scripture is God-breathed and true. When we memorize it, we carry the good news of Jesus with us wherever we go.

Therefore, our God, hear the prayer and the petitions of your servant. Make your face shine on your desolate sanctuary for the Lord's sake. Listen closely, my God, and hear. Open your eyes and see our desolations and the city that bears your name. For we are not presenting our petitions before you based on our righteous acts, but based on your abundant compassion.

DANIEL 9:17–18

Over the course of this study, we will memorize Daniel 9:17–18. Let's begin by memorizing verse 17, the first verse in this prayer of corporate confession.

Write the passage out by hand, say it aloud, or test your knowledge with a friend.

NEBUCHADNEZZAR'S

DAY   08

PROCLAMATION

Daniel 4

¹ King Nebuchadnezzar,

To those of every people, nation, and language, who live on the whole earth:

May your prosperity increase. ² I am pleased to tell you about the miracles and wonders the Most High God has done for me.

> ³ How great are his miracles,
> and how mighty his wonders!
> His kingdom is an eternal kingdom,
> and his dominion is from generation to generation.

THE DREAM

⁴ I, Nebuchadnezzar, was at ease in my house and flourishing in my palace. ⁵ I had a dream, and it frightened me; while in my bed, the images and visions in my mind alarmed me. ⁶ So I issued a decree to bring all the wise men of Babylon to me in order that they might make the dream's interpretation known to me. ⁷ When the magicians, mediums, Chaldeans, and diviners came in, I told them the dream, but they could not make its interpretation known to me.

⁸ Finally Daniel, named Belteshazzar after the name of my god—and a spirit of the holy gods is in him—came before me. I told him the dream: ⁹ "Belteshazzar, head of the magicians, because I know that you have the spirit of the holy gods and that no mystery puzzles you, explain to me the visions of my dream that I saw, and its interpretation. ¹⁰ In the visions of my mind as I was lying in bed, I saw this:

> There was a tree in the middle of the earth,
> and it was very tall.
> ¹¹ The tree grew large and strong;
> its top reached to the sky,
> and it was visible to the ends of the earth.
> ¹² Its leaves were beautiful, its fruit was abundant,
> and on it was food for all.
> Wild animals found shelter under it,
> the birds of the sky lived in its branches,
> and every creature was fed from it.

¹³ "As I was lying in my bed, I also saw in the visions of my mind a watcher, a holy one, coming down from heaven. ¹⁴ He called out loudly:

Cut down the tree and chop off its branches;
strip off its leaves and scatter its fruit.
Let the animals flee from under it,
and the birds from its branches.
[15] But leave the stump with its roots in the ground
and with a band of iron and bronze around it
in the tender grass of the field.
Let him be drenched with dew from the sky
and share the plants of the earth
with the animals.
[16] Let his mind be changed from that of a human,
and let him be given the mind of an animal
for seven periods of time.
[17] This word is by decree of the watchers,
and the decision is by command from the holy ones.
This is so that the living will know
that the Most High is ruler
over human kingdoms.
He gives them to anyone he wants
and sets the lowliest of people over them.

[18] This is the dream that I, King Nebuchadnezzar, had. Now, Belteshazzar, tell me the interpretation, because none of the wise men of my kingdom can make the interpretation known to me. But you can, because you have a spirit of the holy gods."

THE DREAM INTERPRETED

[19] Then Daniel, whose name is Belteshazzar, was stunned for a moment, and his thoughts alarmed him. The king said, "Belteshazzar, don't let the dream or its interpretation alarm you."

Belteshazzar answered, "My lord, may the dream apply to those who hate you, and its interpretation to your enemies! [20] The tree you saw, which grew large and strong, whose top reached to the sky and was visible to the whole earth, [21] and whose leaves were beautiful and its fruit abundant—and on it was food for all, under it the wild animals lived, and in its branches the birds of the sky lived— [22] that tree is you, Your Majesty. For you have become great and strong: your greatness has grown and even reaches the sky, and your dominion extends to the ends of the earth.

[23] "The king saw a watcher, a holy one, coming down from heaven and saying, 'Cut down the tree and destroy it, but leave the stump with its roots in the ground and with a band of iron and bronze around it in the tender grass of the field. Let him

be drenched with dew from the sky and share food with the wild animals for seven periods of time.' [24] This is the interpretation, Your Majesty, and this is the decree of the Most High that has been issued against my lord the king: [25] You will be driven away from people to live with the wild animals. You will feed on grass like cattle and be drenched with dew from the sky for seven periods of time, until you acknowledge that the Most High is ruler over human kingdoms, and he gives them to anyone he wants. [26] As for the command to leave the tree's stump with its roots,

your kingdom will be restored to you as soon as you acknowledge that Heaven rules.

[27] Therefore, may my advice seem good to you my king. Separate yourself from your sins by doing what is right, and from your injustices by showing mercy to the needy. Perhaps there will be an extension of your prosperity."

THE SENTENCE EXECUTED

[28] All this happened to King Nebuchadnezzar. [29] At the end of twelve months, as he was walking on the roof of the royal palace in Babylon, [30] the king exclaimed, "Is this not Babylon the Great that I have built to be a royal residence by my vast power and for my majestic glory?"

[31] While the words were still in the king's mouth, a voice came from heaven: "King Nebuchadnezzar, to you it is declared that the kingdom has departed from you. [32] You will be driven away from people to live with the wild animals, and you will feed on grass like cattle for seven periods of time, until you acknowledge that the Most High is ruler over human kingdoms, and he gives them to anyone he wants."

[33] At that moment the message against Nebuchadnezzar was fulfilled. He was driven away from people. He ate grass like cattle, and his body was drenched with dew from the sky, until his hair grew like eagles' feathers and his nails like birds' claws.

NEBUCHADNEZZAR'S PRAISE

[34] But at the end of those days, I, Nebuchadnezzar, looked up to heaven, and my sanity returned to me. Then I praised the Most High and honored and glorified him who lives forever:

For his dominion is an everlasting dominion,
and his kingdom is from generation to generation.
[35] All the inhabitants of the earth are counted as nothing,
and he does what he wants with the army of heaven

and the inhabitants of the earth.
There is no one who can block his hand
or say to him, "What have you done?"

[36] At that time my sanity returned to me, and my majesty and splendor returned to me for the glory of my kingdom. My advisers and my nobles sought me out, I was reestablished over my kingdom, and even more greatness came to me. [37] Now I, Nebuchadnezzar, praise, exalt, and glorify the King of the heavens, because all his works are true and his ways are just. He is able to humble those who walk in pride.

Proverbs 16:18

Pride comes before destruction,
and an arrogant spirit before a fall.

1 Corinthians 1:28–29

[28] God has chosen what is insignificant and despised in the world—what is viewed as nothing—to bring to nothing what is viewed as something, [29] so that no one may boast in his presence.

Day: 　　　　　　　　　　　**Reading:**

NARRATIVE

TODAY'S READING WAS
(circle one)

A DREAM

The main symbol was

○ A COLOSSAL STATUE

○ A TALL TREE

The Ruler

○ King Nebuchadnezzar of Babylon

○ King Belshazzar of Babylon

○ Darius the Mede

○ King Cyrus of Persia

POINT OF VIEW

○ THIRD PERSON

○ FIRST PERSON

Speaker:

_____

Mentioned by name

○ God

○ Daniel

○ Shadrach

○ Meshach

○ Abednego

○ Chaldeans

○ The Queen

○ Ancient of Days

○ Son of Man

○ Gabriel

○ Michael

What was the

CENTRAL CONFLICT

_____

RESOLUTION

List things said about God or actions that He takes.

DAY 09

THE HANDWRITING ON THE WALL

BUT YOU HAVE NOT GLORIFIED THE GOD WHO HOLDS YOUR LIFE-BREATH IN HIS HAND…

DANIEL 5:23

Daniel 5

BELSHAZZAR'S FEAST

¹ King Belshazzar held a great feast for a thousand of his nobles and drank wine in their presence. ² Under the influence of the wine, Belshazzar gave orders to bring in the gold and silver vessels that his predecessor Nebuchadnezzar had taken from the temple in Jerusalem, so that the king and his nobles, wives, and concubines could drink from them. ³ So they brought in the gold vessels that had been taken from the temple, the house of God in Jerusalem, and the king and his nobles, wives, and concubines drank from them. ⁴ They drank the wine and praised their gods made of gold and silver, bronze, iron, wood, and stone.

THE HANDWRITING ON THE WALL

⁵ At that moment the fingers of a man's hand appeared and began writing on the plaster of the king's palace wall next to the lampstand. As the king watched the hand that was writing, ⁶ his face turned pale, and his thoughts so terrified him that he soiled himself and his knees knocked together. ⁷ The king shouted to bring in the mediums, Chaldeans, and diviners. He said to these wise men of Babylon, "Whoever reads this

inscription and gives me its interpretation will be clothed in purple, have a gold chain around his neck, and have the third highest position in the kingdom." [8] So all the king's wise men came in, but none could read the inscription or make its interpretation known to him. [9] Then King Belshazzar became even more terrified, his face turned pale, and his nobles were bewildered.

[10] Because of the outcry of the king and his nobles, the queen came to the banquet hall. "May the king live forever," she said. "Don't let your thoughts terrify you or your face be pale. [11] There is a man in your kingdom who has a spirit of the holy gods in him. In the days of your predecessor he was found to have insight, intelligence, and wisdom like the wisdom of the gods. Your predecessor, King Nebuchadnezzar, appointed him chief of the magicians, mediums, Chaldeans, and diviners. Your own predecessor, the king, [12] did this because Daniel, the one the king named Belteshazzar, was found to have an extraordinary spirit, knowledge and intelligence, and the ability to interpret dreams, explain riddles, and solve problems. Therefore, summon Daniel, and he will give the interpretation."

DANIEL BEFORE THE KING

[13] Then Daniel was brought before the king. The king said to him, "Are you Daniel, one of the Judean exiles that my predecessor the king brought from Judah? [14] I've heard that you have a spirit of the gods in you, and that insight, intelligence, and extraordinary wisdom are found in you. [15] Now the wise men and mediums were brought before me to read this inscription and make its interpretation known to me, but they could not give its interpretation. [16] However, I have heard about you that you can give interpretations and solve problems. Therefore, if you can read this inscription and give me its interpretation, you will be clothed in purple, have a gold chain around your neck, and have the third highest position in the kingdom."

[17] Then Daniel answered the king, "You may keep your gifts and give your rewards to someone else; however, I will read the inscription for the king and make the interpretation known to him. [18] Your Majesty, the Most High God gave sovereignty, greatness, glory, and majesty to your predecessor Nebuchadnezzar. [19] Because of the greatness he gave him, all peoples, nations, and languages were terrified and fearful of him. He killed anyone he wanted and kept alive anyone he wanted; he exalted anyone he wanted and humbled anyone he wanted. [20] But when his heart was exalted and his spirit became arrogant, he was deposed from his royal throne and his glory was taken from him. [21] He was driven away from people, his mind was like an animal's, he lived with the wild donkeys, he was fed grass like cattle, and his body was drenched with dew from the sky until he acknowledged that the Most High God is ruler over human kingdoms and sets anyone he wants over them.

22 "But you his successor, Belshazzar, have not humbled your heart, even though you knew all this. 23 Instead, you have exalted yourself against the Lord of the heavens. The vessels from his house were brought to you, and as you and your nobles, wives, and concubines drank wine from them, you praised the gods made of silver and gold, bronze, iron, wood, and stone, which do not see or hear or understand.

But you have not glorified the God who holds your life-breath in his hand and who controls the whole course of your life.

24 Therefore, he sent the hand, and this writing was inscribed.

THE INSCRIPTION'S INTERPRETATION

25 "This is the writing that was inscribed: MENE, MENE, TEKEL, and PARSIN. 26 This is the interpretation of the message:

'Mene' means that God has numbered the days of your kingdom and brought it to an end.
27 'Tekel' means that you have been weighed on the balance and found deficient.
28 'Peres' means that your kingdom has been divided and given to the Medes and Persians."

29 Then Belshazzar gave an order, and they clothed Daniel in purple, placed a gold chain around his neck, and issued a proclamation concerning him that he should be the third ruler in the kingdom.

30 That very night Belshazzar the king of the Chaldeans was killed, 31 and Darius the Mede received the kingdom at the age of sixty-two.

1 Peter 5:4–7

4 And when the chief Shepherd appears, you will receive the unfading crown of glory. 5 In the same way, you who are younger, be subject to the elders. All of you clothe yourselves with humility toward one another, because

God resists the proud
but gives grace to the humble.

6 Humble yourselves, therefore, under the mighty hand of God, so that he may exalt you at the proper time, 7 casting all your cares on him, because he cares about you.

1 John 2:15–17

15 Do not love the world or the things in the world. If anyone loves the world, the love of the Father is not in him. 16 For everything in the world—the lust of the flesh, the lust of the eyes, and the pride in one's possessions—is not from the Father, but is from the world. 17 And the world with its lust is passing away, but the one who does the will of God remains forever.

Day: Reading:

NARRATIVE

TODAY'S READING WAS
(circle one)

A DREAM

The main symbol was

○ A COLOSSAL STATUE

○ A TALL TREE

The Ruler

○ King Nebuchadnezzar of Babylon

○ King Belshazzar of Babylon

○ Darius the Mede

○ King Cyrus of Persia

POINT OF VIEW

○ THIRD PERSON

○ FIRST PERSON

Speaker:

_____

Mentioned by name

○ God

○ Daniel

○ Shadrach

○ Meshach

○ Abednego

○ Chaldeans

○ The Queen

○ Ancient of Days

○ Son of Man

○ Gabriel

○ Michael

What was the

CENTRAL CONFLICT

_____

RESOLUTION

Describe the actions, habits, and attitudes of the Babylonian captors and the Hebrew captives.

THE BOOK OF DANIEL IN HISTORY

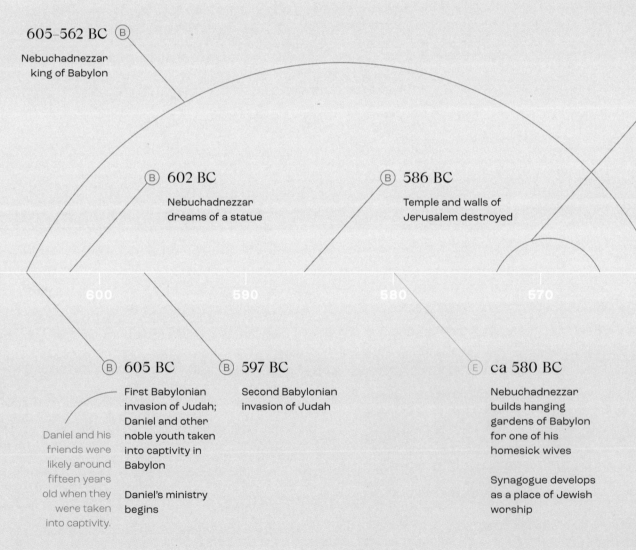

605–562 BC Ⓑ

Nebuchadnezzar
king of Babylon

602 BC Ⓑ

Nebuchadnezzar
dreams of a statue

586 BC Ⓑ

Temple and walls of
Jerusalem destroyed

600

590

580

570

Ⓑ **605 BC**

First Babylonian
invasion of Judah;
Daniel and other
noble youth taken
into captivity in
Babylon

Daniel's ministry
begins

*Daniel and his
friends were
likely around
fifteen years
old when they
were taken
into captivity.*

Ⓑ **597 BC**

Second Babylonian
invasion of Judah

Ⓔ **ca 580 BC**

Nebuchadnezzar
builds hanging
gardens of Babylon
for one of his
homesick wives

Synagogue develops
as a place of Jewish
worship

Ⓑ **573–566 BC**

Nebuchadnezzar's seven
years of insanity

Ⓑ **535 BC**

Daniel's vision of
future events

Ⓑ **552–539 BC**

Belshazzar king
of Babylon

Ⓑ **538 BC**

Cyrus's decree allows
exiles to return to Judah

550   540   530   520

Ⓔ **ca 550 BC**

The game of polo
originates in
Persian Empire

Ⓑ **539 BC**

Belshazzar sees
handwriting on
the wall

Under rule of
King Cyrus,
the kingdom
of Persia
conquers
Babylon

Daniel was
around
eighty-four
years old
when he was
thrown into
the lions' den.

Ⓑ **536 BC**

Daniel thrown into
the lions' den

Ⓔ **534 BC**

Thespis, inventor
of the genre of
tragedy, wins
the first drama
competition at a
festival in Athens

DANIEL IN THE LIONS' DEN

Daniel 6

THE PLOT AGAINST DANIEL

[1] Darius decided to appoint 120 satraps over the kingdom, stationed throughout the realm, [2] and over them three administrators, including Daniel. These satraps would be accountable to them so that the king would not be defrauded. [3] Daniel distinguished himself above the administrators and satraps because he had an extraordinary spirit, so the king planned to set him over the whole realm. [4] The administrators and satraps, therefore, kept trying to find a charge against Daniel regarding the kingdom. But they could find no charge or corruption, for he was trustworthy, and no negligence or corruption was found in him. [5] Then these men said, "We will never find any charge against this Daniel unless we find something against him concerning the law of his God."

[6] So the administrators and satraps went together to the king and said to him, "May King Darius live forever. [7] All the administrators of the kingdom—the prefects, satraps, advisers, and governors—have agreed that the king should establish an ordinance and enforce an edict that, for thirty days, anyone who petitions any god or man except you, the king, will be thrown into the lions' den. [8] Therefore, Your Majesty, establish the edict and sign the document so that, as a law of the Medes and Persians, it is irrevocable and cannot be changed." [9] So King Darius signed the written edict.

DANIEL IN THE LIONS' DEN

[10] When Daniel learned that the document had been signed, he went into his house. The windows in its upstairs room opened toward Jerusalem, and

three times a day he got down on his knees, prayed, and gave thanks to his God, just as he had done before.

[11] Then these men went as a group and found Daniel petitioning and imploring his God. [12] So they approached the king and asked about his edict: "Didn't you sign an edict that for thirty days any person who petitions any god or man except you, the king, will be thrown into the lions' den?"

The king answered, "As a law of the Medes and Persians, the order stands and is irrevocable."

[13] Then they replied to the king, "Daniel, one of the Judean exiles, has ignored you, the king, and the edict you signed, for he prays three times a day." [14] As soon as the king heard this, he was very displeased; he set his mind on rescuing Daniel and made every effort until sundown to deliver him.

[15] Then these men went together to the king and said to him, "You know, Your Majesty, that it is a law of the Medes and Persians that no edict or ordinance the king establishes can be changed."

[16] So the king gave the order, and they brought Daniel and threw him into the lions' den. The king said to Daniel,

"May your God, whom you continually serve, rescue you!"

17 A stone was brought and placed over the mouth of the den. The king sealed it with his own signet ring and with the signet rings of his nobles, so that nothing in regard to Daniel could be changed. 18 Then the king went to his palace and spent the night fasting. No diversions were brought to him, and he could not sleep.

DANIEL RELEASED

19 At the first light of dawn the king got up and hurried to the lions' den. 20 When he reached the den, he cried out in anguish to Daniel. "Daniel, servant of the living God," the king said, "has your God, whom you continually serve, been able to rescue you from the lions?"

21 Then Daniel spoke with the king: "May the king live forever. 22 My God sent his angel and shut the lions' mouths; and they haven't harmed me, for I was found innocent before him. And also before you, Your Majesty, I have not done harm."

23 The king was overjoyed and gave orders to take Daniel out of the den. When Daniel was brought up from the den, he was found to be unharmed, for he trusted in his God. 24 The king then gave the command, and those men who had maliciously accused Daniel were brought and thrown into the lions' den—they, their children, and their wives. They had not reached the bottom of the den before the lions overpowered them and crushed all their bones.

DARIUS HONORS GOD

25 Then King Darius wrote to those of every people, nation, and language who live on the whole earth: "May your prosperity abound. 26 I issue a decree that in all my royal dominion, people must tremble in fear before the God of Daniel:

For he is the living God,
and he endures forever;
his kingdom will never be destroyed,
and his dominion has no end.

27 He rescues and delivers;
he performs signs and
   wonders
in the heavens and on the
   earth,
for he has rescued Daniel
from the power of the lions."

[28] So Daniel prospered during the reign of Darius and the reign of Cyrus the Persian.

2 Timothy 3:12–15

[12] In fact, all who want to live a godly life in Christ Jesus will be persecuted. [13] Evil people and impostors will become worse, deceiving and being deceived. [14] But as for you, continue in what you have learned and firmly believed. You know those who taught you, [15] and you know that from infancy you have known the sacred Scriptures, which are able to give you wisdom for salvation through faith in Christ Jesus.

1 Peter 5:8–9

[8] Be sober-minded, be alert.

Your adversary the devil is prowling around like a roaring lion, looking for anyone he can devour.

[9] Resist him, firm in the faith, knowing that the same kind of sufferings are being experienced by your fellow believers throughout the world.

Day:	Reading:

NARRATIVE

TODAY'S READING WAS
(circle one)

A DREAM

The main symbol was

○ A COLOSSAL STATUE

○ A TALL TREE

The Ruler

○ King Nebuchadnezzar of Babylon

○ King Belshazzar of Babylon

○ Darius the Mede

○ King Cyrus of Persia

POINT OF VIEW

○ THIRD PERSON

○ FIRST PERSON

Speaker:

_____

Mentioned by name

○ God

○ Daniel

○ Shadrach

○ Meshach

○ Abednego

○ Chaldeans

○ The Queen

○ Ancient of Days

○ Son of Man

○ Gabriel

○ Michael

What was the

CENTRAL CONFLICT

_____

RESOLUTION

List things said about God or actions that He takes.

THE ANCIENT OF DAYS

AND THE SON OF MAN

Daniel 7:1–14

DANIEL'S VISION OF THE FOUR BEASTS

¹ In the first year of King Belshazzar of Babylon,

Daniel had a dream with visions in his mind as he was lying in his bed.

He wrote down the dream, and here is the summary of his account. ² Daniel said, "In my vision at night I was watching, and suddenly the four winds of heaven stirred up the great sea. ³ Four huge beasts came up from the sea, each different from the other.

⁴ "The first was like a lion but had eagle's wings. I continued watching until its wings were torn off. It was lifted up from the ground, set on its feet like a man, and given a human mind.

⁵ "Suddenly, another beast appeared, a second one, that looked like a bear. It was raised up on one side, with three ribs in its mouth between its teeth. It was told, 'Get up! Gorge yourself on flesh.'

⁶ "After this, while I was watching, suddenly another beast appeared. It was like a leopard with four wings of a bird on its back. It had four heads, and it was given dominion.

⁷ "After this, while I was watching in the night visions, suddenly a fourth beast appeared, frightening and dreadful, and incredibly strong, with large iron teeth. It devoured and crushed, and it trampled with its feet whatever was left. It was different from all the beasts before it, and it had ten horns.

⁸ "While I was considering the horns, suddenly another horn, a little one, came up among them, and three of the first horns were uprooted before it. And suddenly in this horn there were eyes like the eyes of a human and a mouth that was speaking arrogantly.

THE ANCIENT OF DAYS AND THE SON OF MAN

⁹ "As I kept watching,

thrones were set in place,
and the Ancient of Days took his seat.

His clothing was white like snow,
and the hair of his head like whitest wool.
His throne was flaming fire;
its wheels were blazing fire.
¹⁰ A river of fire was flowing,
coming out from his presence.
Thousands upon thousands served him;
ten thousand times ten thousand stood before him.
The court was convened,
and the books were opened.

¹¹ "I watched, then, because of the sound of the arrogant words the horn was speaking. As I continued watching, the beast was killed and its body destroyed and given over to the burning fire. ¹² As for the rest of the beasts, their dominion was removed, but an extension of life was granted to them for a certain period of time. ¹³ I continued watching in the night visions,

and suddenly one like a son of man
was coming with the clouds of heaven.
He approached the Ancient of Days
and was escorted before him.
¹⁴ He was given dominion
and glory and a kingdom,
so that those of every people,
nation, and language
should serve him.
His dominion is an everlasting dominion
that will not pass away,
and his kingdom is one
that will not be destroyed."

Psalm 104:1–5

GOD THE CREATOR

¹ My soul, bless the LORD!
LORD my God, you are very great;
you are clothed with majesty and splendor.
² He wraps himself in light as if it were a robe,
spreading out the sky like a canopy,
³ laying the beams of his palace
on the waters above,

making the clouds his chariot,
walking on the wings of the wind,
⁴ and making the winds his messengers,
flames of fire his servants.

⁵ He established the earth on its foundations;
it will never be shaken.

Hebrews 12:28–29

²⁸ Therefore, since we are receiving a kingdom that cannot be shaken, let us be thankful.

By it, we may serve God acceptably, with reverence and awe, ²⁹ for our God is a consuming fire.

Day:	Reading:

NARRATIVE · A DREAM

TODAY'S READING WAS
(circle one)

A VISION

POINT OF VIEW

○ THIRD PERSON

○ FIRST PERSON

Speaker:

_____

The Ruler

○ King Nebuchadnezzar of Babylon

○ King Belshazzar of Babylon

○ Darius the Mede

○ King Cyrus of Persia

Mentioned by name

○ God

○ Daniel

○ Shadrach

○ Meshach

○ Abednego

○ Chaldeans

○ The Queen

○ Ancient of Days

○ Son of Man

○ Gabriel

○ Michael

AN IMAGE THAT STUCK OUT TO ME
FROM THE READING:

Where was Daniel when he received the vision?

_____

SYMBOLS IN THE VISION

○ Winds

○ Huge beasts

○ The sea

○ Lion with eagle's wings

○ Bear with _____ ribs in its mouth

○ Leopard with _____ wings and _____ heads

○ Beast with iron teeth and _____ horns

○ Little horn

○ Horns

○ Broken horns

○ Throne with wheels

○ River of fire

○ Ram with _____ horns

○ Goat

○ Abomination of desolation

○ Warrior king

○ Other:

_____

_____

_____

_____

_____

THE SON OF MAN

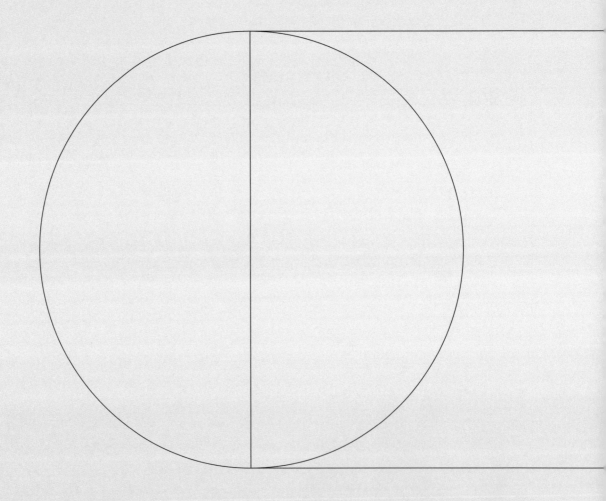

In chapter 7, Daniel sees a vision of the "son of man," one like a human being, appearing before the throne of the Ancient of Days. As the vision progresses, this son of man is shown to be more than just an ordinary human. He is a figure of hope and triumph, exalted and not defeated, who reigns with God. In the Gospels, Jesus repeatedly refers to Himself as the Son of Man, confirming that this passage is a prophecy about the Messiah. Here are just some of the connections made between the New Testament and this pivotal messianic passage.

I continued watching in the night visions,

and suddenly one
like a son of man
was coming with the clouds of heaven.
He approached the
Ancient
of
Days
and was escorted
before him.

Jesus refers to Himself as the Son of Man more than any other term or title. Mt 11:18–19; 16:27–28; Mk 10:33; Lk 9:58; Jn 1:51; 6:53; 9:35–37; 12:34

Mt 24:30; Mk 13:26; 14:62; Ac 1:9; Rv 14:14

The only time "Son of Man" is proclaimed as a title by someone other than Jesus is when Stephen, dying as a martyr, cries out, "I see the heavens opened and the Son of Man standing at the right hand of God!" Ac 7:56

Paul alludes to this vision when he writes about what Christ accomplished on our behalf. Php 2:6–9

He was given dominion
and glory
and a kingdom,
so that those of every
people,
nation,
and language
should serve him.

Lk 5:24; Jn 3:35; 1Co 15:27; Eph 1:20–22; Rv 1:6

Jesus taught that His glory is intricately bound up with His suffering on the cross and resurrection. Mt 20:18–19; 25:31; Mk 8:31; 13:26; Lk 9:44; 18:31–33; Jn 3:14–15; 12:23–24, 34; 13:31

Rv 7:9–17

His dominion is
an everlasting dominion
that will
not pass
a
w
a
y,

Heb 12:28; Rv 11:15

Gabriel, the angel who interprets Daniel's visions in chapters 8 and 9, is referred to by name two other times in Scripture. In the book of Luke, he promises the birth of John the Baptist. Later, he tells Mary that she will become pregnant, and that her child will be this promised Son of Man who will reign forever over a kingdom that has no end. Dn 8; 9; Lk 1

and his kingdom is one that will not
be
destroyed.
...

As I was watching, this horn
waged war against the holy
ones and was prevailing over
them until the Ancient of Days
arrived and a judgment was
given in favor of the holy ones
of the Most High, for the time
had come, and the holy ones
took possession of the kingdom.

Lk 19:10; Jn 5:27; 6:27; 8:28
...

The kingdom, dominion, and
greatness of the kingdoms
under all of heaven will be
given to the people, the holy
ones of the Most High. His
kingdom will be an everlasting
kingdom, and all rulers will
serve and obey him.

Rv 20:4

INTERPRETATION OF THE VISION

BUT THE HOLY ONES OF THE MOST HIGH WILL RECEIVE THE KINGDOM AND POSSESS IT FOREVER.

DANIEL 7:18

Daniel 7:15–28

INTERPRETATION OF THE VISION

[15] "As for me, Daniel, my spirit was deeply distressed within me, and the visions in my mind terrified me. [16] I approached one of those who were standing by and asked him to clarify all this. So he let me know the interpretation of these things: [17] 'These huge beasts, four in number, are four kings who will rise from the earth. [18] But the holy ones of the Most High will receive the kingdom and possess it forever, yes, forever and ever.'

[19] "Then I wanted to be clear about the fourth beast, the one different from all the others, extremely terrifying, with iron teeth and bronze claws, devouring, crushing, and trampling with its feet whatever was left. [20] I also wanted to know about the ten horns on its head and about the other horn that came up, before which three fell—the horn that had eyes, and a mouth that spoke arrogantly, and that looked bigger than the others. [21] As I was watching, this horn waged war against the holy ones and was prevailing over them [22] until the Ancient of Days arrived and a judgment was given in favor of the holy ones of the Most High, for the time had come, and the holy ones took possession of the kingdom.

23 "This is what he said: 'The fourth beast will be a fourth kingdom on the earth, different from all the other kingdoms. It will devour the whole earth, trample it down, and crush it. 24 The ten horns are ten kings who will rise from this kingdom. Another king, different from the previous ones, will rise after them and subdue three kings. 25 He will speak words against the Most High and oppress the holy ones of the Most High. He will intend to change religious festivals and laws, and the holy ones will be handed over to him for a time, times, and half a time. 26 But the court will convene, and his dominion will be taken away, to be completely destroyed forever. 27 The kingdom, dominion, and greatness of the kingdoms under all of heaven will be given to the people, the holy ones of the Most High.

His kingdom will be an everlasting kingdom, and all rulers will serve and obey him.'

28 "This is the end of the account. As for me, Daniel, my thoughts terrified me greatly, and my face turned pale, but I kept the matter to myself."

Philippians 4:6–7

6 Don't worry about anything, but in everything, through prayer and petition with thanksgiving, present your requests to God. 7 And the peace of God, which surpasses all understanding, will guard your hearts and minds in Christ Jesus.

Colossians 1:15–20

THE CENTRALITY OF CHRIST

15 He is the image of the invisible God,
the firstborn over all creation.

16 For everything was created
  by him,
in heaven and on earth,
the visible and the invisible,
whether thrones or dominions
or rulers or authorities—

all things have been created through him and for him.
[17] He is before all things,
and by him all things hold together.
[18] He is also the head of the body, the church;
he is the beginning,
the firstborn from the dead,
so that he might come to have
first place in everything.
[19] For God was pleased to have
all his fullness dwell in him,
[20] and through him to reconcile
everything to himself,
whether things on earth or things in heaven,
by making peace
through his blood, shed on the cross.

Day:	Reading:

NARRATIVE · A DREAM · A VISION

TODAY'S READING WAS
(circle one)

POINT OF VIEW

○ THIRD PERSON

○ FIRST PERSON

Speaker:

_____

The Ruler

○ King Nebuchadnezzar of Babylon

○ King Belshazzar of Babylon

○ Darius the Mede

○ King Cyrus of Persia

Mentioned by name

○ God

○ Daniel

○ Shadrach

○ Meshach

○ Abednego

○ Chaldeans

○ The Queen

○ Ancient of Days

○ Son of Man

○ Gabriel

○ Michael

AN IMAGE THAT STUCK OUT TO ME FROM THE READING:

How did Daniel respond to the vision? Who did Daniel ask to help him understand it?

_____

SYMBOLS IN THE VISION

○ Winds

○ Huge beasts

○ The sea

○ Lion with eagle's wings

○ Bear with _____ ribs in its mouth

○ Leopard with _____ wings and _____ heads

○ Beast with iron teeth and _____ horns

○ Little horn

○ Horns

○ Broken horns

○ Throne with wheels

○ River of fire

○ Ram with _____ horns

○ Goat

○ Abomination of desolation

○ Warrior king

○ Other:

_____

_____

_____

_____

_____

GRACE DAY

DAY 13

Take this day to catch up on your reading, pray, and rest in the presence of the Lord.

Don't worry about anything, but in everything, through prayer and petition with thanksgiving, present your requests to God.

PHILIPPIANS 4:6

WEEKLY TRUTH

Scripture is God-breathed and true. When
we memorize it, we carry the good news of
Jesus with us wherever we go.

Therefore, our God,
hear the prayer and the
petitions of your servant.
Make your face shine on
your desolate sanctuary
for the Lord's sake. Listen
closely, my God, and hear.
Open your eyes and see
our desolations and the
city that bears your name.
For we are not presenting
our petitions before you
based on our righteous
acts, but based on your
abundant compassion.

DANIEL 9:17–18

This week, we will build on what we
memorized last week by focusing on the
first part of verse 18 from Daniel's prayer.

Write the passage out by hand, say it aloud,
or test your knowledge with a friend.

THE VISION OF A RAM AND A GOAT

Daniel 8

THE VISION OF A RAM AND A GOAT

[1] In the third year of King Belshazzar's reign, a vision appeared to me, Daniel, after the one that had appeared to me earlier. [2] I saw the vision, and as I watched, I was in the fortress city of Susa, in the province of Elam. I saw in the vision that I was beside the Ulai Canal. [3] I looked up, and there was a ram standing beside the canal. He had two horns. The two horns were long, but one was longer than the other, and the longer one came up last. [4] I saw the ram charging to the west, the north, and the south. No animal could stand against him, and there was no rescue from his power. He did whatever he wanted and became great.

[5] As I was observing, a male goat appeared, coming from the west across the surface of the entire earth without touching the ground. The goat had a conspicuous horn between his eyes. [6] He came toward the two-horned ram I had seen standing

beside the canal and rushed at him with savage fury. [7] I saw him approaching the ram, and infuriated with him, he struck the ram, breaking his two horns, and the ram was not strong enough to stand against him. The goat threw him to the ground and trampled him, and there was no one to rescue the ram from his power. [8] Then the male goat acted even more arrogantly, but when he became powerful, the large horn was broken. Four conspicuous horns came up in its place, pointing toward the four winds of heaven.

THE LITTLE HORN

[9] From one of them a little horn emerged and grew extensively toward the south and the east and toward the beautiful land. [10] It grew as high as the heavenly army, made some of the army and some of the stars fall to the earth, and trampled them. [11] It acted arrogantly even against the Prince of the heavenly army; it revoked his regular sacrifice and overthrew the place of his sanctuary. [12] In the rebellion, the army was given up, together with the regular sacrifice. The horn threw truth to the ground and was successful in what it did.

[13] Then I heard a holy one speaking, and another holy one said to the speaker, "How long will the events of this vision last—the regular sacrifice, the rebellion that makes desolate, and the giving over of the sanctuary and of the army to be trampled?"

[14] He said to me, "For 2,300 evenings and mornings; then the sanctuary will be restored."

INTERPRETATION OF THE VISION

[15] While I, Daniel, was watching the vision and trying to understand it, there stood before me someone who appeared to be a man. [16] I heard a human voice calling from the middle of the Ulai: "Gabriel, explain the vision to this man."

[17] So he approached where I was standing; when he came near, I was terrified and fell facedown.

"Son of man," he said to me, "understand that the vision refers to the time of the end."

[18] While he was speaking to me, I fell into a deep sleep, with my face to the ground. Then he touched me, made me stand up, [19] and said, "I am here to tell you what will happen at the conclusion of the time of wrath, because it refers to the appointed time of the end. [20] The two-horned ram that you saw represents the

kings of Media and Persia. [21] The shaggy goat represents the king of Greece, and the large horn between his eyes represents the first king. [22] The four horns that took the place of the broken horn represent four kingdoms. They will rise from that nation, but without its power.

[23] Near the end of their kingdoms,
when the rebels have reached
the full measure of their sin,
a ruthless king, skilled in intrigue,
will come to the throne.

[24] His power will be great, but it will not be his own.

He will cause outrageous destruction
and succeed in whatever he does.
He will destroy the powerful
along with the holy people.
[25] He will cause deceit to prosper
through his cunning and by his influence,
and in his own mind he will exalt himself.
He will destroy many in a time of peace;
he will even stand against the Prince of princes.
Yet he will be broken—not by human hands.
[26] The vision of the evenings and the mornings
that has been told is true.
Now you are to seal up the vision
because it refers to many days in the future."

[27] I, Daniel, was overcome and lay sick for days. Then I got up and went about the king's business. I was greatly disturbed by the vision and could not understand it.

Isaiah 6:1–7

ISAIAH'S CALL AND MISSION

[1] In the year that King Uzziah died, I saw the Lord seated on a high and lofty throne, and the hem of his robe filled the temple. [2] Seraphim were standing above him; they each had six wings: with two they covered their faces, with two they covered their feet, and with two they flew. [3] And one called to another:

Holy, holy, holy is the LORD of Armies;
his glory fills the whole earth.

⁴ The foundations of the doorways shook at the sound of their voices, and the temple was filled with smoke.

⁵ Then I said:

> Woe is me for I am ruined
> because I am a man of unclean lips
> and live among a people of unclean lips,
> and because my eyes have seen the King,
> the LORD of Armies.

⁶ Then one of the seraphim flew to me, and in his hand was a glowing coal that he had taken from the altar with tongs. ⁷ He touched my mouth with it and said:

> Now that this has touched your lips,
> your iniquity is removed
> and your sin is atoned for.

Romans 8:31–39

THE BELIEVER'S TRIUMPH

³¹ What, then, are we to say about these things? If God is for us, who is against us? ³² He did not even spare his own Son but gave him up for us all. How will he not also with him grant us everything? ³³ Who can bring an accusation against God's elect? God is the one who justifies. ³⁴ Who is the one who condemns? Christ Jesus is the one who died, but even more, has been raised; he also is at the right hand of God and intercedes for us. ³⁵ Who can separate us from the love of Christ? Can affliction or distress or persecution or famine or nakedness or danger or sword? ³⁶ As it is written:

> Because of you
> we are being put to death all day long;
> we are counted as sheep to be slaughtered.

³⁷ No, in all these things we are more than conquerors through him who loved us. ³⁸ For I am persuaded that neither death nor life, nor angels nor rulers, nor things present nor things to come, nor powers, ³⁹ nor height nor depth, nor any other created thing will be able to separate us from the love of God that is in Christ Jesus our Lord.

Day:	Reading:

NARRATIVE · A DREAM · A VISION

TODAY'S READING WAS
(circle one)

POINT OF VIEW

○ THIRD PERSON

○ FIRST PERSON

Speaker:

_____

The Ruler

○ King Nebuchadnezzar of Babylon

○ King Belshazzar of Babylon

○ Darius the Mede

○ King Cyrus of Persia

Mentioned by name

○ God

○ Daniel

○ Shadrach

○ Meshach

○ Abednego

○ Chaldeans

○ The Queen

○ Ancient of Days

○ Son of Man

○ Gabriel

○ Michael

AN IMAGE THAT STUCK OUT TO ME
FROM THE READING:

Who explained this vision to Daniel?

_____

SYMBOLS IN THE VISION

○ Winds

○ Huge beasts

○ The sea

○ Lion with eagle's wings

○ Bear with _____ ribs in its mouth

○ Leopard with _____ wings and _____ heads

○ Beast with iron teeth and _____ horns

○ Little horn

○ Horns

○ Broken horns

○ Throne with wheels

○ River of fire

○ Ram with _____ horns

○ Goat

○ Abomination of desolation

○ Warrior king

○ Other:

_____

_____

_____

_____

_____

_____

In the second chapter of the book of Daniel, King Nebuchadnezzar dreams of a statue that is destroyed by a rock. Later, in chapters 7 and 8, Daniel himself receives a series of visions connected to Nebuchadnezzar's dream. Here is a summary of the dream and visions and what each represents.

NEBUCHADNEZZAR'S DREAM	DANIEL'S VISIONS	REPRESENTED
The statue has a head of pure gold. 2:31–32, 36–38	A lion with eagle's wings 7:3–4	THE BABYLONIAN EMPIRE
The statue's chest and arms are made of silver. 2:32, 39	A bear raised up on one side with three ribs in its mouth 7:5 A ram with two horns 8:3–4, 20	THE MEDO-PERSIAN EMPIRE (or Media)
The statue has an abdomen and thighs made of bronze. 2:32, 39	A leopard with four wings and four heads 7:6 A goat with four horns growing from broken horns 8:5–12, 21–25	THE GREEKS, ALEXANDER THE GREAT AND HIS FOUR SUCCESSORS (or Persia)
The statue's legs are made of iron, and its feet are iron baked in clay. 2:33, 40–43	A wild beast with iron teeth and ten horns on its head 7:7–8, 23–25	THE ROMAN EMPIRE (or Greece)
A rock, uncut by human hands, smashes the statue and becomes a huge mountain, filling the earth. 2:34–35, 44–45	The Ancient of Days gives the Son of Man, who comes on the clouds of heaven, the authority to rule an everlasting kingdom. 7:9–14, 26–27	THE BIRTH OF JESUS AND THE KINGDOM OF GOD

DANIEL'S PRAYER

Daniel 9

DANIEL'S PRAYER

¹ In the first year of Darius, the son of Ahasuerus, a Mede by birth, who was made king over the Chaldean kingdom— ² in the first year of his reign, I, Daniel, understood from the books according to the word of the LORD to the prophet Jeremiah that the number of years for the desolation of Jerusalem would be seventy. ³ So I turned my attention to the Lord God to seek him by prayer and petitions, with fasting, sackcloth, and ashes.

⁴ I prayed to the LORD my God and confessed:

Ah, Lord—the great and awe-inspiring God who keeps his gracious covenant with those who love him and keep his commands— ⁵ we have sinned, done wrong, acted wickedly, rebelled, and turned away from your commands and ordinances. ⁶ We have not listened to your servants the prophets, who spoke in your name to our kings, leaders, ancestors, and all the people of the land.

7 Lord, righteousness belongs to you,

but this day public shame belongs to us: the men of Judah, the residents of Jerusalem, and all Israel—those who are near and those who are far, in all the countries where you have banished them because of the disloyalty they have shown toward you. 8 LORD, public shame belongs to us, our kings, our leaders, and our ancestors, because we have sinned against you. 9 Compassion and forgiveness belong to the Lord our God, though we have rebelled against him 10 and have not obeyed the LORD our God by following his instructions that he set before us through his servants the prophets.

11 All Israel has broken your law and turned away, refusing to obey you. The promised curse written in the law of Moses, the servant of God, has been poured out on us because we have sinned against him. 12 He has carried out his words that he spoke against us and against our rulers by bringing on us a disaster that is so great that nothing like what has been done to Jerusalem has ever been done under all of heaven. 13 Just as it is written in the law of Moses, all this disaster has come on us, yet we have not sought the favor of the LORD our God by turning from our iniquities and paying attention to your truth. 14 So the LORD kept the disaster in mind and brought it on us, for the LORD our God is righteous in all he has done. But we have not obeyed him.

15 Now, Lord our God—who brought your people out of the land of Egypt with a strong hand and made your name renowned as it is this day—we have sinned, we have acted wickedly. 16 Lord, in keeping with all your righteous acts, may your anger and wrath turn away from your city Jerusalem, your holy mountain; for because of our sins and the iniquities of our ancestors, Jerusalem and your people have become an object of ridicule to all those around us.

17 Therefore, our God, hear the prayer and the petitions of your servant.

Make your face shine on your desolate sanctuary for the Lord's sake.

18 Listen closely, my God, and hear. Open your eyes and see our desolations and the city that bears your name. For we are not presenting our petitions before you based on our righteous acts, but based on your abundant compassion. 19 Lord, hear! Lord, forgive! Lord, listen and act! My God, for your own sake, do not delay, because your city and your people bear your name.

²⁰ While I was speaking, praying, confessing my sin and the sin of my people Israel, and presenting my petition before the Lᴏʀᴅ my God concerning the holy mountain of my God— ²¹ while I was praying, Gabriel, the man I had seen in the first vision, reached me in my extreme weariness, about the time of the evening offering. ²² He gave me this explanation: "Daniel, I've come now to give you understanding. ²³ At the beginning of your petitions an answer went out, and I have come to give it, for you are treasured by God. So consider the message and understand the vision:

²⁴ Seventy weeks are decreed
about your people and your holy city—
to bring the rebellion to an end,
to put a stop to sin,
to atone for iniquity,
to bring in everlasting righteousness,
to seal up vision and prophecy,
and to anoint the most holy place.
²⁵ Know and understand this:
From the issuing of the decree
to restore and rebuild Jerusalem
until an Anointed One, the ruler,
will be seven weeks and sixty-two weeks.
It will be rebuilt with a plaza and a moat,
but in difficult times.
²⁶ After those sixty-two weeks
the Anointed One will be cut off
and will have nothing.
The people of the coming ruler
will destroy the city and the sanctuary.
The end will come with a flood,
and until the end there will be war;
desolations are decreed.
²⁷ He will make a firm covenant
with many for one week,
but in the middle of the week
he will put a stop to sacrifice and offering.
And the abomination of desolation
will be on a wing of the temple
until the decreed destruction
is poured out on the desolator."

1 Kings 9:6–9

⁶ If you or your sons turn away from following me and do not keep my commands—my statutes that I have set before you—and if you go and serve other gods and bow in worship to them, ⁷ I will cut off Israel from the land I gave them, and I will reject the temple I have sanctified for my name. Israel will become an object of scorn and ridicule among all the peoples. ⁸ Though this temple is now exalted, everyone who passes by will be appalled and will scoff. They will say, "Why did the Lᴏʀᴅ do this to this land and this temple?" ⁹ Then they will say, "Because they abandoned the Lᴏʀᴅ their God who brought their ancestors out of the land of Egypt. They held on to other gods and bowed in worship to them and served them. Because of this, the Lᴏʀᴅ brought all this ruin on them."

Ephesians 2:1–5

FROM DEATH TO LIFE

¹ And you were dead in your trespasses and sins ² in which you previously lived according to the ways of this world, according to the ruler of the power of the air, the spirit now working in the disobedient. ³ We too all previously lived among them in our fleshly desires, carrying out the inclinations of our flesh and thoughts, and we were by nature children under wrath as the others were also.

⁴ But God, who is rich in mercy, because of his great love that he had for us, ⁵ made us alive with Christ

even though we were dead in trespasses. You are saved by grace!

Day:	Reading:

NARRATIVE · A DREAM · A VISION

TODAY'S READING WAS
(circle one)

POINT OF VIEW

○ THIRD PERSON

○ FIRST PERSON

Speaker:

_____

The Ruler

○ King Nebuchadnezzar of Babylon

○ King Belshazzar of Babylon

○ Darius the Mede

○ King Cyrus of Persia

Mentioned by name

○ God

○ Daniel

○ Shadrach

○ Meshach

○ Abednego

○ Chaldeans

○ The Queen

○ Ancient of Days

○ Son of Man

○ Gabriel

○ Michael

AN IMAGE THAT STUCK OUT TO ME FROM THE READING:

Which biblical prophet did Daniel rely on to interpret his vision?

_____

SYMBOLS IN THE VISION

○ Winds

○ Huge beasts

○ The sea

○ Lion with eagle's wings

○ Bear with _____ ribs in its mouth

○ Leopard with _____ wings and _____ heads

○ Beast with iron teeth and _____ horns

○ Little horn

○ Horns

○ Broken horns

○ Throne with wheels

○ River of fire

○ Ram with _____ horns

○ Goat

○ Abomination of desolation

○ Warrior king

○ Other:

_____

_____

_____

_____

_____

ANGELIC

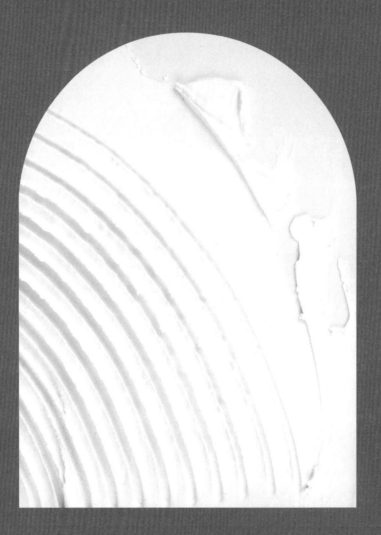

CONFLICT

Daniel 10

VISION OF A GLORIOUS ONE

¹ In the third year of King Cyrus of Persia, a message was revealed to Daniel, who was named Belteshazzar. The message was true and was about a great conflict. He understood the message and had understanding of the vision.

² In those days I, Daniel, was mourning for three full weeks. ³ I didn't eat any rich food, no meat or wine entered my mouth, and I didn't put any oil on my body until the three weeks were over. ⁴ On the twenty-fourth day of the first month, as I was standing on the bank of the great river, the Tigris, ⁵ I looked up, and there was a man dressed in linen, with a belt of gold from Uphaz around his waist. ⁶ His body was like beryl, his face like the brilliance of lightning, his eyes like flaming torches, his arms and feet like the gleam of polished bronze, and the sound of his words like the sound of a multitude.

⁷ Only I, Daniel, saw the vision. The men who were with me did not see it, but a great terror fell on them, and they ran and hid. ⁸ I was left alone, looking at this great vision. No strength was left in me; my face grew deathly pale, and I was powerless. ⁹ I heard the words he said, and when I heard them I fell into a deep sleep, with my face to the ground.

ANGELIC CONFLICT

¹⁰ Suddenly, a hand touched me and set me shaking on my hands and knees. ¹¹ He said to me,

"Daniel, you are a man treasured by God.

Understand the words that I'm saying to you. Stand on your feet, for I have now been sent to you." After he said this to me, I stood trembling.

¹² "Don't be afraid, Daniel," he said to me, "for from the first day that you purposed to understand and to humble yourself before your God, your prayers were heard. I have come because of your prayers. ¹³ But the prince of the kingdom of Persia opposed me for twenty-one days. Then Michael, one of the chief princes, came to help me after I had been left there with the kings of Persia. ¹⁴ Now I have come to help you understand what will happen to your people in the last days, for the vision refers to those days."

¹⁵ While he was saying these words to me, I turned my face toward the ground and was speechless. ¹⁶ Suddenly one with human likeness touched my lips. I opened my mouth and said to the one standing in front of me, "My lord, because of the vision, anguish overwhelms me and I am powerless. ¹⁷ How can someone like me,

your servant, speak with someone like you, my lord? Now I have no strength, and there is no breath in me."

[18] Then the one with a human appearance touched me again and strengthened me. [19] He said, "Don't be afraid, you who are treasured by God. Peace to you; be very strong!"

As he spoke to me, I was strengthened and said, "Let my lord speak, for you have strengthened me."

[20] He said, "Do you know why I've come to you? I must return at once to fight against the prince of Persia, and when I leave, the prince of Greece will come. [21] However, I will tell you what is recorded in the book of truth. (No one has the courage to support me against those princes except Michael, your prince."

Daniel 11:1–4

[1] In the first year of Darius the Mede, I stood up to strengthen and protect him.)
[2] Now I will tell you the truth.

PROPHECIES ABOUT PERSIA AND GREECE

"Three more kings will arise in Persia, and the fourth will be far richer than the others. By the power he gains through his riches, he will stir up everyone against the kingdom of Greece. [3] Then a warrior king will arise; he will rule a vast realm and do whatever he wants. [4] But as soon as he is established, his kingdom will be broken up and divided to the four winds of heaven, but not to his descendants; it will not be the same kingdom that he ruled, because his kingdom will be uprooted and will go to others besides them."

2 Corinthians 10:3–5

[3] For although we live in the flesh, we do not wage war according to the flesh, [4] since the weapons of our warfare are not of the flesh, but are powerful through God for the demolition of strongholds. We demolish arguments [5] and every proud thing that is raised up against the knowledge of God, and we take every thought captive to obey Christ.

Ephesians 6:12

For our struggle is not against flesh and blood, but against the rulers, against the authorities, against the cosmic powers of this darkness, against evil, spiritual forces in the heavens.

Day:	Reading:

NARRATIVE · A DREAM · A VISION

TODAY'S READING WAS
(circle one)

POINT OF VIEW

○ THIRD PERSON

○ FIRST PERSON

Speaker:

_____

The Ruler

○ King Nebuchadnezzar of Babylon

○ King Belshazzar of Babylon

○ Darius the Mede

○ King Cyrus of Persia

Mentioned by name

○ God

○ Daniel

○ Shadrach

○ Meshach

○ Abednego

○ Chaldeans

○ The Queen

○ Ancient of Days

○ Son of Man

○ Gabriel

○ Michael

AN IMAGE THAT STUCK OUT TO ME FROM THE READING:

What was Daniel doing as he mourned and prayed?

_____

SYMBOLS IN THE VISION

○ Winds

○ Huge beasts

○ The sea

○ Lion with eagle's wings

○ Bear with _____ ribs in its mouth

○ Leopard with _____ wings and _____ heads

○ Beast with iron teeth and _____ horns

○ Little horn

○ Horns

○ Broken horns

○ Throne with wheels

○ River of fire

○ Ram with _____ horns

○ Goat

○ Abomination of desolation

○ Warrior king

○ Other:

_____

_____

_____

_____

_____

KINGS OF THE SOUTH AND THE NORTH

Daniel 11:5–45

KINGS OF THE SOUTH AND THE NORTH

[5] "The king of the South will grow powerful, but one of his commanders will grow more powerful and will rule a kingdom greater than his. [6] After some years they will form an alliance, and the daughter of the king of the South will go to the king of the North to seal the agreement. She will not retain power, and his strength will not endure. She will be given up, together with her entourage, her father, and the one who supported her during those times. [7] In the place of the king of the South, one from her family will rise up, come against the army, and enter the fortress of the king of the North. He will take action against them and triumph. [8] He will take even their gods captive to Egypt, with their metal images and their precious articles of silver and gold. For some years he will stay away from the king of the North, [9] who will enter the kingdom of the king of the South and then return to his own land.

¹⁰ "His sons will mobilize for war and assemble a large number of armed forces. They will advance, sweeping through like a flood, and will again wage war as far as his fortress. ¹¹ Infuriated, the king of the South will march out to fight with the king of the North, who will raise a large army, but they will be handed over to his enemy. ¹² When the army is carried off, he will become arrogant and cause tens of thousands to fall, but he will not triumph. ¹³ The king of the North will again raise a multitude larger than the first. After some years he will advance with a great army and many supplies.

¹⁴ "In those times many will rise up against the king of the South. Violent ones among your own people will assert themselves to fulfill a vision, but they will fail. ¹⁵ Then the king of the North will come, build up a siege ramp, and capture a well-fortified city. The forces of the South will not stand; even their select troops will not be able to resist. ¹⁶ The king of the North who comes against him will do whatever he wants, and no one can oppose him. He will establish himself in the beautiful land with total destruction in his hand. ¹⁷ He will resolve to come with the force of his whole kingdom and will reach an agreement with him. He will give him a daughter in marriage to destroy it, but she will not stand with him or support him. ¹⁸ Then he will turn his attention to the coasts and islands and capture many. But a commander will put an end to his taunting; instead, he will turn his taunts against him. ¹⁹ He will turn his attention back to the fortresses of his own land, but he will stumble, fall, and be no more.

²⁰ "In his place one will arise who will send out a tax collector for the glory of the kingdom; but within a few days he will be broken, though not in anger or in battle.

²¹ "In his place a despised person will arise; royal honors will not be given to him, but he will come during a time of peace and seize the kingdom by intrigue. ²² A flood of forces will be swept away before him; they will be broken, as well as the covenant prince. ²³ After an alliance is made with him, he will act deceitfully. He will rise to power with a small nation. ²⁴ During a time of peace, he will come into the richest parts of the province and do what his fathers and predecessors never did. He will lavish plunder, loot, and wealth on his followers, and he will make plans against fortified cities, but only for a time.

²⁵ "With a large army he will stir up his power and his courage against the king of the South. The king of the South will prepare for battle with an extremely large and powerful army, but he will not succeed, because plots will be made against him. ²⁶ Those who eat his provisions will destroy him; his army will be swept away, and many will fall slain. ²⁷ The two kings, whose hearts are bent on evil, will speak lies at the same table but to no avail, for still the end will come at the appointed time. ²⁸ The king of the North will return to his land with great wealth, but his heart will be set against the holy covenant; he will take action, then return to his own land.

²⁹ "At the appointed time he will come again to the South, but this time will not be like the first. ³⁰ Ships of Kittim will come against him, and being intimidated, he will withdraw. Then he will rage against the holy covenant and take action. On his return, he will favor those who abandon the holy covenant. ³¹ His forces will rise up and desecrate the temple fortress. They will abolish the regular sacrifice and set up the abomination of desolation. ³² With flattery he will corrupt those who act wickedly toward the covenant,

but the people who know their God will be strong and take action.

³³ Those who have insight among the people will give understanding to many, yet they will fall by the sword and flame, and they will be captured and plundered for a time. ³⁴ When they fall, they will be helped by some, but many others will join them insincerely. ³⁵ Some of those who have insight will fall so that they may be refined, purified, and cleansed until the time of the end, for it will still come at the appointed time.

³⁶ "Then the king will do whatever he wants. He will exalt and magnify himself above every god, and he will say outrageous things against the God of gods. He will be successful until the time of wrath is completed, because what has been decreed will be accomplished. ³⁷ He will not show regard for the gods of his ancestors, the god desired by women, or for any other god, because he will magnify himself above all. ³⁸ Instead, he will honor a god of fortresses—a god his ancestors did not know—with gold, silver, precious stones, and riches. ³⁹ He will deal with the strongest fortresses with the help of a foreign god. He will greatly honor those who acknowledge him, making them rulers over many and distributing land as a reward.

⁴⁰ "At the time of the end, the king of the South will engage him in battle, but the king of the North will storm against him with chariots, horsemen, and many ships. He will invade countries and sweep through them like a flood. ⁴¹ He will also invade the beautiful land, and many will fall. But these will escape from his power: Edom, Moab, and the prominent people of the Ammonites. ⁴² He will extend his power against the countries, and not even the land of Egypt will escape. ⁴³ He will get control over the hidden treasures of gold and silver and over all the riches of Egypt. The Libyans and Cushites will also be in submission. ⁴⁴ But reports from the east and the north will terrify him, and he will go out with great fury to annihilate and completely destroy many. ⁴⁵ He will pitch his royal tents between the sea and the beautiful holy mountain, but he will meet his end with no one to help him."

Ezekiel 20:4–9

[4] "Will you pass judgment against them, will you pass judgment, son of man? Explain the detestable practices of their ancestors to them. [5] Say to them, 'This is what the Lord God says: On the day I chose Israel, I swore an oath to the descendants of Jacob's house and made myself known to them in the land of Egypt. I swore to them, saying, "I am the Lord your God." [6] On that day I swore to them that I would bring them out of the land of Egypt into a land I had searched out for them, a land flowing with milk and honey, the most beautiful of all lands. [7] I also said to them, "Throw away, each of you, the abhorrent things that you prize, and do not defile yourselves with the idols of Egypt. I am the Lord your God."

[8] "'But they rebelled against me and were unwilling to listen to me. None of them threw away the abhorrent things that they prized, and they did not abandon the idols of Egypt. So I considered pouring out my wrath on them, exhausting my anger against them within the land of Egypt. [9] But I acted for the sake of my name, so that it would not be profaned in the eyes of the nations they were living among, in whose sight I had made myself known to Israel by bringing them out of Egypt.'"

Matthew 23:37–39

[37] "Jerusalem, Jerusalem, who kills the prophets and stones those who are sent to her. How often I wanted to gather your children together, as a hen gathers her chicks under her wings, but you were not willing! [38] See, your house is left to you desolate. [39] For I tell you, you will not see me again until you say, 'Blessed is he who comes in the name of the Lord'!"

Day:	Reading:

NARRATIVE   A DREAM

TODAY'S READING WAS
(circle one)

A VISION

POINT OF VIEW

- ○ THIRD PERSON
- ○ FIRST PERSON

Speaker:

_____

The Ruler

- ○ King Nebuchadnezzar of Babylon
- ○ King Belshazzar of Babylon
- ○ Darius the Mede
- ○ King Cyrus of Persia

Mentioned by name

- ○ God
- ○ Daniel
- ○ Shadrach
- ○ Meshach
- ○ Abednego
- ○ Chaldeans
- ○ The Queen
- ○ Ancient of Days
- ○ Son of Man
- ○ Gabriel
- ○ Michael

AN IMAGE THAT STUCK OUT TO ME
FROM THE READING:

Look back at yesterday's reading (10:4). Where was Daniel when he received this vision?

_____

SYMBOLS IN THE VISION

- ○ Winds
- ○ Huge beasts
- ○ The sea
- ○ Lion with eagle's wings
- ○ Bear with _____ ribs in its mouth
- ○ Leopard with _____ wings and _____ heads
- ○ Beast with iron teeth and _____ horns

- ○ Little horn
- ○ Horns
- ○ Broken horns
- ○ Throne with wheels
- ○ River of fire
- ○ Ram with _____ horns
- ○ Goat
- ○ Abomination of desolation

- ○ Warrior king
- ○ Other:

_____

_____

_____

_____

_____

COME, THOU

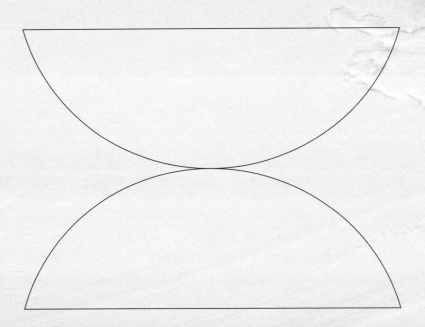

ALMIGHTY KING

WORDS: ANONYMOUS
MUSIC: FELICE DE GIARDINI

DAY 19

THE END OF DAYS

Daniel 12:1–13

[1] At that time
Michael, the great prince
who stands watch over your people, will rise up.
There will be a time of distress
such as never has occurred
since nations came into being until that time.
But at that time all your people
who are found written in the book will escape.
[2] Many who sleep in the dust
of the earth will awake,
some to eternal life,
and some to disgrace and eternal contempt.
[3] Those who have insight will shine
like the bright expanse of the heavens,
and those who lead many to righteousness,
like the stars forever and ever.

⁴ "But you, Daniel, keep these words secret and seal the book until the time of the end. Many will roam about, and knowledge will increase."

⁵ Then I, Daniel, looked, and two others were standing there, one on this bank of the river and one on the other. ⁶ One of them said to the man dressed in linen, who was above the water of the river,

"How long until the end of these wondrous things?"

⁷ Then I heard the man dressed in linen, who was above the water of the river. He raised both his hands toward heaven and swore by him who lives eternally that it would be for a time, times, and half a time. When the power of the holy people is shattered, all these things will be completed.

⁸ I heard but did not understand. So I asked, "My lord, what will be the outcome of these things?"

⁹ He said, "Go on your way, Daniel, for the words are secret and sealed until the time of the end. ¹⁰ Many will be purified, cleansed, and refined, but the wicked will act wickedly; none of the wicked will understand, but those who have insight will understand. ¹¹ From the time the daily sacrifice is abolished and the abomination of desolation is set up, there will be 1,290 days. ¹² Happy is the one who waits for and reaches 1,335 days. ¹³ But as for you, go on your way to the end; you will rest, and then you will rise to receive your allotted inheritance at the end of the days."

2 Peter 3:8–13

⁸ Dear friends, don't overlook this one fact: With the Lord one day is like a thousand years, and a thousand years like one day. ⁹ The Lord does not delay his promise, as some understand delay, but is patient with you, not wanting any to perish but all to come to repentance.

¹⁰ But the day of the Lord will come like a thief; on that day the heavens will pass away with a loud noise, the elements will burn and be dissolved, and the earth and the works on it will be disclosed. ¹¹ Since all these things are to be dissolved in this way, it is clear what sort of people you should be in holy conduct and godliness ¹² as you wait for the day of God and hasten its coming. Because of that day, the heavens will be dissolved with fire and the elements will melt with heat. ¹³ But based on his promise, we wait for new heavens and a new earth, where righteousness dwells.

Revelation 1:4–8

[4] John: To the seven churches in Asia. Grace and peace to you from the one who is, who was, and who is to come, and from the seven spirits before his throne, [5] and from Jesus Christ, the faithful witness, the firstborn from the dead and the ruler of the kings of the earth.

To him who loves us and has set us free from our sins by his blood, [6] and made us a kingdom, priests to his God and Father—to him be glory and dominion forever and ever. Amen.

[7] Look, he is coming with the clouds,
and every eye will see him,
even those who pierced him.

And all the tribes of the earth
will mourn over him.
So it is to be. Amen.

[8] "I am the Alpha and the Omega," says the Lord God, "the one who is, who was, and who is to come, the Almighty."

Day:	Reading:

NARRATIVE A DREAM

TODAY'S READING WAS
(circle one)

A VISION

POINT OF VIEW

○ THIRD PERSON

○ FIRST PERSON

Speaker:

_____

The Ruler

○ King Nebuchadnezzar of Babylon

○ King Belshazzar of Babylon

○ Darius the Mede

○ King Cyrus of Persia

Mentioned by name

○ God
○ Daniel
○ Shadrach
○ Meshach
○ Abednego
○ Chaldeans

○ The Queen
○ Ancient of Days
○ Son of Man
○ Gabriel
○ Michael

AN IMAGE THAT STUCK OUT TO ME
FROM THE READING:

How does Daniel respond to these visions?

_____

SYMBOLS IN THE VISION

○ Winds

○ Huge beasts

○ The sea

○ Lion with eagle's wings

○ Bear with ____ ribs in its mouth

○ Leopard with ____ wings and ____ heads

○ Beast with iron teeth and ____ horns

○ Little horn

○ Horns

○ Broken horns

○ Throne with wheels

○ River of fire

○ Ram with ____ horns

○ Goat

○ Abomination of desolation

○ Warrior king

○ Other:

_____

_____

_____

_____

_____

GRACE DAY

DAY 20

Take this day to catch up on your reading, pray, and rest in the presence of the Lord.

But God, who is rich in mercy, because of his great love that he had for us, made us alive with Christ....

EPHESIANS 2:4–5

WEEKLY TRUTH

Scripture is God-breathed and true. When we memorize it, we carry the good news of Jesus with us wherever we go.

Therefore, our God, hear the prayer and the petitions of your servant. Make your face shine on your desolate sanctuary for the Lord's sake. Listen closely, my God, and hear. Open your eyes and see our desolations and the city that bears your name. For we are not presenting our petitions before you based on our righteous acts, but based on your abundant compassion.

DANIEL 9:17–18

For our final week, we will finish memorizing the last verse in this passage from Daniel. Here, the prophet expresses humility before God and seeks His compassion.

Write the passage out by hand, say it aloud, or test your knowledge with a friend.

PRAYER OF
CONFESSION

THEREFORE,
        our God, hear the prayer and
            the petitions of your servant.
Make your face
      s
        h
          i
            n
              e
            on your desolate sanctuary
            for the Lord's sake.
Listen closely,
        my God,
            and hear.
Open your eyes
        and see our desolations
        and the city that
            bears your name.
For we are not
        presenting
            our petitions
              before you
              based on our
              righteous acts,
            but based on
              your abundant
              compassion.
Lord, hear!
Lord, forgive!
Lord, listen and act!

My God,
        for your own sake,
        do not delay,
            because your city
            and your people
              bear your name.

              DANIEL 9:17–19

DOWNLOAD THE APP

VISIT
shereadstruth.com

SHOP
shopshereadstruth.com

CONTACT
hello@shereadstruth.com

CONNECT
@shereadstruth
#shereadstruth

LISTEN
She Reads Truth Podcast

CSB BOOK ABBREVIATIONS

OLD TESTAMENT

Genesis – Gn
Exodus – Ex
Leviticus – Lv
Numbers – Nm
Deuteronomy – Dt
Joshua – Jos
Judges – Jdg
Ruth – Ru
1 Samuel – 1Sm
2 Samuel – 2Sm
1 Kings – 1Kg
2 Kings – 2Kg
1 Chronicles – 1Ch
2 Chronicles – 2Ch
Ezra – Ezr
Nehemiah – Neh
Esther – Est
Job – Jb
Psalms – Ps
Proverbs – Pr
Ecclesiastes – Ec
Song of Solomon – Sg

Isaiah – Is
Jeremiah – Jr
Lamentations – Lm
Ezekiel – Ezk
Daniel – Dn
Hosea – Hs
Joel – Jl
Amos – Am
Obadiah – Ob
Jonah – Jnh
Micah – Mc
Nahum – Nah
Habakkuk – Hab
Zephaniah – Zph
Haggai – Hg
Zechariah – Zch
Malachi – Mal

NEW TESTAMENT

Matthew – Mt
Mark – Mk
Luke – Lk
John – Jn

Acts – Ac
Romans – Rm
1 Corinthians – 1Co
2 Corinthians – 2Co
Galatians – Gl
Ephesians – Eph
Philippians – Php
Colossians – Col
1 Thessalonians – 1Th
2 Thessalonians – 2Th
1 Timothy – 1Tm
2 Timothy – 2Tm
Titus – Ti
Philemon – Phm
Hebrews – Heb
James – Jms
1 Peter – 1Pt
2 Peter – 2Pt
1 John – 1Jn
2 John – 2Jn
3 John – 3Jn
Jude – Jd
Revelation – Rv

BIBLIOGRAPHY

Baldwin, Joyce G. Daniel: *An Introduction and Commentary*. Vol. 23, *Tyndale Old Testament Commentaries*. Downers Grove: InterVarsity Press, 1978.

Beck, John A. *The Baker Book of Bible Charts, Maps, and Time Lines*. Ada: Baker Books, 2016. *Faithlife Study Bible*. Grand Rapids: Zondervan, 2017.

Longman, Tremper, and J. Daniel Hays. *Message of the Prophets: A Survey of the Prophetic and Apocalyptic Books of the Old Testament*. Grand Rapids: Zondervan, 2010.

Miller, Stephen. *Daniel: An Exegetical and Theological Exposition of Holy Scripture. Vol 18, The New American Commentary*. B&H Publishing Group: Nashville, 1994.

Peter-Contesse, Rene, and John Ellington. *A Handbook on the Book of Daniel: UBS Handbook Series*. New York: United Bible Societies, 1993.

SHE READS TRUTH

Inspired by the She Reads Truth mission of "Women in the Word of God every day," the *She Reads Truth Bible* is thoughtfully and artfully designed to highlight the beauty, goodness, and truth found in Scripture.

FEATURES

- Custom reading plans to help you navigate your time in the Word

- Thoughtful devotionals throughout each book of the Bible

- Maps, charts, and timelines to provide context and Scripture connections

- 66 hand-lettered key verses to aid in Scripture memorization

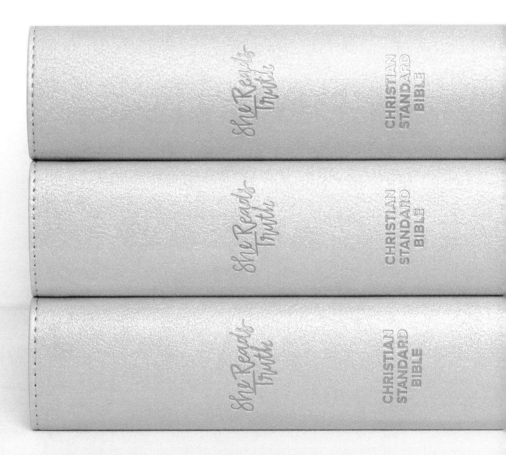

USE CODE SRTB15 FOR 15% OFF YOUR NEW SHE READS TRUTH BIBLE!

SHOPSHEREADSTRUTH.COM

READY FOR YOUR NEXT STEP?

At She Reads Truth, we have one simple but powerful mission: women in the Word of God every day. To support this mission, we offer a variety of resources and tools to enhance your time in God's Word.

SHE READS TRUTH PODCAST

Join us in a weekly conversation with our founders, Raechel and Amanda, as they explore the beauty, goodness, and truth of Scripture. The She Reads Truth podcast serves as a companion resource to the She Reads Truth reading plans, Study Books, and devotionals.

Join us on Apple Podcasts or your preferred streaming platform.

SHE READS TRUTH APP

You'll find daily devotional responses for every Bible reading plan we create on the She Reads Truth app. You can also read the Bible, participate in community discussions, download lock screens for Scripture memorization, and more! Join women from Portland to Poland as they read Truth alongside you.

Download on the App Store or Google Play.

SHEREADSTRUTH.COM

All of our reading plans and devotionals are free at SheReadsTruth.com! This is an easy, convenient way to invite your family, friends, and neighbors to read God's Word with you.

WHERE DID I STUDY?

O HOME

O OFFICE

O COFFEE SHOP

O CHURCH

O A FRIEND'S HOUSE

O OTHER:

WHAT WAS I LISTENING TO?

ARTIST:

SONG:

PLAYLIST:

WHEN DID I STUDY?

MORNING

AFTERNOON

NIGHT

HOW DID I FIND DELIGHT IN GOD'S WORD?

WHAT WAS HAPPENING IN MY LIFE?

WHAT WAS HAPPENING IN THE WORLD?

| MONTH | DAY | YEAR |

END DATE